Teaching in a Networked Classroom

The pace of technological change has made the   ...uate and long-term future difficult, if not impossible, to predict. Teachers are forced to imagine the world they are preparing their students to live in. In this situation, creativity becomes a vital resource for enabling uncertain futures to be embraced, and an important attribute for students to have both for their learning and their employability in the future.

In this book, the authors argue that creativity is a social and collaborative process that can be enhanced through online and digital technologies. Filled with case studies and practical tasks, it shows teachers how they can develop an approach to teaching and learning with digital technologies that is inherently social, collaborative and creative. Including case studies and practical examples of projects and lessons throughout, the chapters cover:

- Learning in a networked society;

- An examination of sharing practices and how knowledge can be shared more effectively;

- Potential pitfalls of virtual learning environments and public social networking sites;

- Using digital media to plan schemes of work and lessons;

- How to facilitate meaningful collaboration and discussion through digital media;

- Creating online environments to enable students to share their understandings and learning.

Bringing together key ideas about creativity, collaborative learning and ICT in the classroom, this timely book will be an invaluable resource for all teachers.

Jonathan Savage is a Reader in Education at the Institute of Education, Manchester Metropolitan University, UK. He is also Managing Director of UCan Play, a company that supports the innovative use of technology in education.

Clive McGoun is a Senior Lecturer in Communication at Manchester Metropolitan University, UK.

Teaching in a Networked Classroom

Jonathan Savage and Clive McGoun

 Routledge
Taylor & Francis Group

LONDON AND NEW YORK

First published 2015
by Routledge
2 Park Square, Milton Park, Abingdon, Oxon OX14 4RN

and by Routledge
711 Third Avenue, New York, NY 10017

Routledge is an imprint of the Taylor & Francis Group, an informa business

British Library Cataloguing in Publication Data
A catalogue record for this book is available from the British Library

Library of Congress Cataloging in Publication Data
Savage, Jonathan.
Teaching in a networked classroom / Jonathan Savage and Clive McGoun.
pages cm
Includes bibliographical references and index.
1. Education--Computer network resources. 2. Teaching--Computer network resources. 3. Internet in education. 4. Web-based instruction. I. McGoun, Clive. II. Title.
LB1044.87.S28 2015
371.33'44678--dc23
2014046358

ISBN: 978-0-415-70897-5 (hbk)
ISBN: 978-0-415-70898-2 (pbk)
ISBN: 978-1-315-69774-1 (ebk)

Typeset in Melior
by Saxon Graphics Ltd, Derby

Printed and bound by CPI Group (UK) Ltd, Croydon, CR0 4YY

Contents

Introduction

For the past three years in the beautiful setting of Edale in the Peak District, over 100 spoon carvers have gathered to share their expertise, enthusiasm and passion for greenwood carving. Over three days they carve together: in workshops, where they concentrate on specific aspects of carving, and on short courses, where the more experienced pass on their skills and understanding. Ninety-nine percent of these people are amateurs, people who become obsessed about something and spend an inordinate amount of time thinking about it and talking about it. In Edale, there is a quiet, contagious enthusiasm. There is an egalitarianism between the most and the least experienced based on an understanding that, even for the few full-time wood carvers, the best way to develop is to maintain the amateur spirit, a Zen-like 'beginner's mind' that sees things as always fresh and new, pregnant with possibilities.

This is a community of people bound by a common passion, where learning takes place through participation. Everyone is immersed in this community during the three days. It quickly becomes clear that, directly or indirectly, everybody knows everybody else. When I was interested to find out who was forging their own tools, I asked Geoff, who I had been carving with near the main tent: 'I don't know, but ask Charlie, I'm sure he'll point you in the right direction.' He did. Friends of friends became my friends. I was definitely a node in a network and my connections were expanding. I carved with Steve from Cumbria. I watched him over and over again axing out a spoon blank, establishing the right 'crank' to make the spoon suitable for the mouth and aesthetically pleasing to the eye. There was a discipline to the carving and every cut made was an instance of that discipline. Steve was modelling good practice. I practised and practised, trying to copy what he was doing. I reflected on the results and tried to work out why and how my spoon blanks lacked his fluent lines, which expressed confidence and style.

We talked. He guided me in modifying my technique with the axe. The learning activity was a conversation, and it added to many such conversations and learning activities that I enjoyed over the three days. My conversation with Steve was with an expert carver. Yet as important were subsequent conversations with the community where I repeated what I learnt, passed it on, and helped others as Steve had helped me. This idea of teaching what you know was deeply embedded in this community. Communities are not add-ons or adjuncts to learning; communities are the learning.

The design principles that guided the learning at Spoonfest were tacit yet very simple: we learn by doing and everyone can participate. There were children as young as six or seven carving with razor-sharp knives. There were complete novices learning how to use an axe and people who, after a lifetime carving, were learning new techniques with new tools. All were challenging themselves in producing a spoon that satisfied them. This inclusive, cross-generational learning context was something very new to me. Rarely had I seen it so naturally and successfully expressed in formal education (where I have spent my professional life) as it was in the context of Spoonfest.

Carving with very sharp knives involves intense concentration. There is a bell that rings at Spoonfest at 6 pm, which means 'Down tools, no more carving'. Tiredness causes cuts. That tiredness comes from the intense concentration. Looking around at the way people in a field could be so absorbed in carving spoons, I was reminded of the concept of 'flow' described by Mihaly Csikszentmihalyi (1990). In his book, and in the TED talk he gave in 2008, Csikszentmihalyi examines that state, which he calls 'flow', where people are so involved in an activity that nothing else seems to matter; where people do something simply for the sake of doing it.[1]

After interviewing thousands of people about their experiences of being fully absorbed in an activity, he concluded that there are several important characteristics of this experience of being in flow. These include:

- Complete concentration on the task;

- The task must have a chance of being completed;

- Clear goals and immediate feedback on progress;

- A merging of actions with awareness so that we become what we do;

- Control over what we are doing without worrying about failure;

- Awareness of self-retreats; we become un-self-conscious;

- Time has no duration; it runs neither slowly nor quickly.

It seemed to me that this was the experience of many people over the three-day weekend in Edale. How did they manage to get into that 'state'? Again, summarising Csikszentmihalyi (selectively for the purposes of understanding more about this community), nobody was carving for societal reward; there was no expectation of payment for the spoons they were making; even seemingly mundane processes were experienced as 'optimal', as intensely joyous. Csikszentmihalyi also talks of people in flow as able to combine 'differentiation' and 'integration'. Whilst differentiation refers to the movement towards the self and our uniqueness, integration is the union with others, with ideas and entities that are beyond us. Many spoon makers did not strictly need to be sitting together deeply concentrating on carving, lost in their world. But they were, at the same time, communing with others. Moments of pause, of reflection, of learning were communally shared moments, which reached beyond the purely individual, unique experience of the activity. This definitely was not work; but it was not play either. It was serious fun and creative, collaborative labour. And nobody wanted it to end.

Now, with the advent of the internet, such groups can continue to gather together, sharing and learning online. The Facebook group 'Spoon Carving, Green Woodworking and Sloyd' quickly became the surrogate online space for the field in Edale. It is used to show carved pieces, ask for advice, share views and news, post video instruction ideas, and curate material related to spoons and their carving. Enthusiasm is constant. Feedback is responsive, supportive and sensitive. Many carvers publish their own blogs and these link together, adding depth to Facebook comments and discussions. These hubs foster engagement not by 'pushing' a particular point of view or product, but simply because they allow people who have a shared interest to easily access resources that will enable them to learn more about what they are interested in improving; and there is always the promise of another meeting together in the field in Edale.

As my interest in spoon carving was being nurtured by these conversations, I began bookmarking sites where green woodworking was discussed. I joined other people who also bookmarked such sites and learnt from them, adding their bookmarks to my own. I searched terms such as 'spoon carving', 'sloyd', 'learning to carve'. I began following blogs written by carvers, jumping from one blogger's list of the blogs they followed to another's, all the time expanding my own sources of information. I watched online videos, bookmarking many and creating a playlist that I could return to. Some carvers used Twitter, so I began reading them, following and un-following them according to how well they contributed to my own interests. With so much information available and constantly changing, I needed a way to make accessing and following it easier. I initially used Google Reader, but when that service closed down I moved to Feedly, an application for web browsers and mobile devices.

Feedly allows me to read the things I am interested in quickly and effectively. I do not read everything. Some things I scan, others I save for a moment when I have time to really enjoy them. I leave comments on blogs where I feel I have something to contribute. I share many articles on Twitter and occasionally use my own blog to write a post about spoons and carving.

What I created here is what many people in an educational context refer to as a 'personal learning network' or PLN. It is my own network of online collaborators (consciously or unconsciously so) who support my learning and with whom I share my interests in and experiences of woodcraft. I have been aided in developing this network by Howard Rheingold's advice on how to build a personal learning network, which he shared in 2011 through eight short tweets:

- Explore: it is not just about knowing how to find experts, co-learners, but about exploration to serendipitous encounter;

- Search: use Diigo, Delicious, Listorius to find pools of expertise in the fields that interest you;

- Follow candidates through RSS, Twitter. Ask yourselves over days and weeks whether each candidate merits continued attention;

- Always keep tuning your network, dropping people who don't gain sufficiently high interest; adding new candidates;

- Feed the people who follow you if you come across information that you suspect would interest them;

- Engage the people you follow. Be mindful of making demands on their attention;

- Enquire of the people you follow, of the people who follow you;

- Respond to enquiries made to you. Contribute to both diffuse reciprocity and quid pro quo.[2]

We recount this story of carving spoons here because in so many ways it frames our interests in writing this book. It reminds us of what learning can look like and, in fact, increasingly looks like for hundreds of thousands of people who are immersed in learning what they are interested in, supported by like-minded people, in networks of mutual interest. These networks are radically open, inclusive and sustained through shared interest. Learning happens in communities through the relationships that are built with the people who can model those things we want to learn or the artefacts we want to produce. Because it is impossible to predict the learning path, learning activities always have the potential to be multi-disciplinary. For example, a desire to paint carved wooden spoons can lead to an exploration of how to mix linseed oil emulsion paint using raw eggs and natural pigment. Sharpening tools can open a door to a world of water stones, diamond whetstones and honing compounds. That multi-disciplinary knowledge is contained in the network and accessed when needed. Creative labour, not workaday drudgery, drives this learning, which, like Stephen Hawking's turtles, is collaborative 'all the way down'.

I might have been carving wooden spoons in a field in Edale, but from that story it is clear that the internet now plays a crucial role in the learning that both informed it and developed from it. This is the internet of 2015, not 2001, when it was seen as synonymous with 'computer technology'. For many people the internet has now left the desktop and become as much a part of our countryside and living rooms as the air we breathe. Desktops are morphing into smartphones and tablets, hard disks are being replaced by the Cloud, and the mouse is giving way to gestures on a touch screen. Very soon, we may be wearing our computers or looking at the world directly through them.

Carving in a field or walking through a city (at least in the United Kingdom) is no reason to disconnect. Stopping for a coffee and not having fast broadband wireless connection is similar to not having sugar or the opportunity to eat a croissant. Nor do we think any more of 'logging on or off'. The various journeys we make are mapped seamlessly onto internet access points in a way that allows us to melt into those connections. It is only when we forget our network ID or password and we are confronted with 'Not connected – Connections are available', that we feel the separation of the online/offline, and we feel lost, bereft of our connections. If in 2001, I logged on to read something published 'online' (a term that is sounding increasingly 'ancient'), in 2014 I am more likely to take a photo on my phone which is uploaded to my network, where it can be shared by my peer group, friends, and friends' friends. The internet is now omnipresent, invisible and relational.

The rise of the internet in the past fifteen years has been accompanied by a story of how innovation, particularly digital and network innovation, changes organisations and industries. 'Innovation' has become a post 9/11 word to describe the way change happens. Instead of talking about 'progress', we talk about innovation, about 'the new'. It is not difficult to find critics of the idea that the world is progressing towards becoming a fairer, kinder, more equitable place. We may have eradicated many contagious diseases, but we are also witnesses to world wars, genocide and seemingly intractable conflict. Hardly progress. Innovation carries with it no such baggage. It is the idea of progress without the problems, of doing things better. The idea of 'disruptive innovation' (Christensen 1997) has been used to describe the ways in which technologies radically change the industries into which they are introduced. This is the process whereby some kind of innovation introduced into a market (for example, car rentals, or book-selling) transforms it by making the services or products offered simpler, easier to access and less expensive. As argued by Christensen, such innovation is a positive force for change. Governments have been anxious to realign their ministerial departments to shape policies in ways that reflect this popular theory of change. In 2007 the Department for Innovation, Universities and Skills in the UK was created to pull together some of the functions of the Department of Education and Skills and the Department of Trade and Industry. In 2009, those departments were officially merged into the Department for Business Innovation and Skills, 'the department for economic growth'.

If innovation is the door to progress and positive change, then creativity has become the key to open that door. Over the past decade we have been inundated with books, websites, consultants and life coaches eager to explain in theoretical and practical terms how to be creative so that we can innovate in our professional and personal lives. Here's a flavour of these ideas in a government report published in 2006:

> Work in the modern British economy will increasingly involve creativity and innovation as a mass and everyday activity, applied not just to leading edge high-tech and cultural industries, but to retailing and services, manufacturing and sales. Britain will need an education system that encourages widespread development of generic skills of creativity which include: idea generation; creative teamwork, opportunity sensing; pitching and auditioning; giving criticism and responding to it; mobilising people and resources around ideas to make them real... (DCMS 2006: 4)

'The modern British economy' is clearly changing and many aspects of it are being reorganised. In place of large corporations, there are increasing numbers of smaller companies coming together into networks to share expertise and increase their influence. This can be seen in school organisation, where more and more schools are joining to form 'network enterprises' (often in the legal form of Educational Trusts) to take advantage of alliances, partnerships and collaboration. This is a world where information and knowledge sharing are key – where new projects share workers, and resource sharing and innovation are driven by creativity.

Of course, it is not only in the world of work where this imperative of innovation and creativity holds sway. Personal creativity is seen as a goal for the 'good life'. We are envious of those creative souls who seem able to banish the banal and boring from their lives and live instead in the present of perpetual discovery. The 'artists', the 'creative types', those are the people we traditionally understood as living meaningful and rewarding lives. It was a small elite. Recently, however, opportunities for personal creativity have been expanding as the barriers to participation have been tumbling. Largely through the advent of digital tools and public communication networks, creativity has become democratised. No longer simply consumers, we are increasingly becoming producers able to share our creations on a global platform. Clearly, these ideas have enormous implications for education.

For example, we now have the freedom to learn anywhere, at any time and at any speed. A new 'culture of learning' (Thomas and Brown 2011) supports bottom-up peer exploration and play. The top-down, teacher-centred instructional model is seen as increasingly anachronistic. This is a model that emerged as a response to the industrial revolution. That revolution demanded standard processes to produce standard products, and formal, compulsory schooling was organised in its image. Where the assembly line processed industrial products, schools have been processing children to standard specifications through age-linked curricula and examinations that mirror quality control mechanisms. In such a system, the transition to work was made seamless; the child, schooled in a factory system, was prepared for work in a factory system. As we move further and further away from such a system of work, so we begin to question the nature of schooling and how it might be best organised to reflect the world we live in now.

It is no longer the case that we go to school to access information that otherwise would be unavailable to us. We can now access information and expertise outside the environments that we find ourselves in, creating and interacting with geographically dispersed communities that nurture our interests and develop our passions. Even our ideas about what knowledge actually is in this world is beginning to change. We are beginning to explore the notion that knowledge in networked communities is more than the sum of its parts, and that it is perhaps in our connections that knowledge is actually generated. What we know (or can remember) at a particular moment in time may be far less important than what and who we are connected with. Many young people who have grown up digitally connected know this intimately. Few schools, however, integrate such understanding into the ways they organise formal learning for such young people.

Finally, the internet is enabling people to personalise their learning according to their needs, wants and whims. We are organising our own 'curricula' with our own learning goals and criteria for success and situating these alongside other commitments in our lives. And we are doing so with other people. With the mass adoption of digital media technologies, it has never been easier to connect to other people, create groups and get things done (Shirky 2008). Learning communities where people are pursuing personal and collective goals are expanding beyond what institutional organisations are able to offer. New ways of collaborating and cooperating are emerging because of these organising possibilities. We really can learn with and from each other.

This book looks in detail at a range of ideas that have informed these new ways of learning enabled by the internet. Those wider ideas are important as they situate many of the discussions about what kind of schooling we could be building today and what kinds of teachers we should be trying to be. Of course, there are some fault lines in the debate. Some argue that the disruption will be so radical that schools will cease to exist in their current institutional form. As Dale Stephens suggests:

> The systems and institutions that we see around us – of schools, college, and work – are being systematically dismantled ... If you want to learn the skills required to navigate the world – the hustle, networking, and creativity – you're going to have to hack your own education. (Stephens 2013: 9)

This is more than an argument for home schooling. DIY (or DIO, do-it-ourselves) education has developed momentum in the past five years, particularly in higher education where costs/debts are skyrocketing (Kamenetz 2010). It looks set to continue with the proliferation of mass open online courses (MOOCs) and open education resources. The less radical position on the fault line argues not for laying aside all current institutional schooling, but for 're-schooling'. This is the idea that we should be aligning schools more closely with digital learners, online learning and the connections that are now possible within, between and beyond the physical institution we call school. Over the past ten years, many educational initiatives have been explored to examine how pedagogy and curricula could be modified to engage with this new world of learning (Bonk 2009; Collins 2009; November 2012).

Our intentions in this book are not to produce a definitive guide on how to 'hack' your own or others' education. Nor is it to provide detailed pedagogical proposals and curricula outlines for re-schooling our current institutions. Instead, our goal is to unpack the ideas that inform these two responses to the changes we are living through, whilst at the same time asking you to reflect on some of the implications for your own work. We hope it provides you with an opportunity to rethink how we all might make teaching and learning in our schools more relevant, not only to today's young people, but also to society. Here is a chapter-by-chapter preview of the book.

Chapter 1 explores some current understandings of creativity, firstly from within the educational establishment, and secondly through the eyes of a group of rather eclectic writers and artists. The discussion will help you to rethink what being creative means and how your own learning and teaching might be modified to incorporate this new view.

Chapter 2 examines how creativity is embedded in networks and how digital networks are increasingly informing and shaping so many aspects of our daily lives. We introduce a theory of learning that has emerged as a response to this proliferation of networks and the implications of this theory for the skills that are needed for learning in the twenty-first century.

Central to the idea of creativity and to learning networks is sharing what you do. In Chapter 3 we take a broad look at what sharing means, why it is important, and why it is becoming more common. With the internet providing so much to potentially share, we then look at how we can take the principles of sharing into learning through the activity of curating resources. It will encourage you to build your own personal learning network and will suggest a range of tools to help you do this productively. Using a metaphor of 'connectiveness', it considers how basic activities such as reading and writing can all be transformed through a networked approach to teaching and learning.

Chapter 4 continues to explore the impact on your work as a teacher of the key concepts and processes drawn from earlier in the book. It also considers how your teaching style and role can be enhanced in more general ways. Finally, it looks at the importance of constructive partnerships at the heart of a networked approach.

Chapter 5 adopts a more sceptical tone. It explores the metaphor of 'technological solutionism' and considers the downside of such a rapid pace of technological change within our society and the implications of this for our educational system. We are not techno-phobic! But we do believe it is important to maintain a balanced approach and fully understand both the affordances and the limitations of the tools we choose to use within our work as teachers.

Chapter 6 is our concluding chapter. In it, we provide an overview of the key messages of the book, before exploring a simple framework of educational evaluation that you might want to adopt to move your work forward in this area. This will help you apply some of the key messages of this book to your own work in a structured way.

So, within the confines of an isolated physical book, written and published on that old technology – paper – but which relates to the inter-connected, networked world of the web – read on!

Notes

1   See blog.ted.com/2008/10/23/creativity_fulf
2   Howard Rheingold's Twitter handle is @hrheingold. These tweets were curated by Alex Howard into Storify at: storify.com/digiphile/how-to-build-a-personal-learning-network-on-twitte

References

Bonk, C. J. (2009). *The World is Open: How web technology is revolutionizing education.* San Francisco, CA, Jossey-Bass.

Csikszentmihalyi, M. (1990). *Flow: The psychology of optimal experience.* New York, Harper & Row.

Christensen, C. M. (1997) *The Innovator's Dilemma: When new technologies cause great firms to fail.* Watertown, MA, Harvard Business Review Press.

Collins, A. H. R. (2009). *Rethinking education in the age of technology: The digital revolution and schooling in America.* New York, Teachers College Press.

DCMS (2006). *Nurturing Creativity in Young People: A report to government to inform future policy.* London, Department for Culture, Media and Sport.

Kamenetz, A. (2010). *DIY U: Edupunks, edupreneurs, and the coming transformation of higher education.* White River Junction, VT, Chelsea Green.

November, A. C. (2012). *Who owns the learning? Preparing students for success in the digital age.* Bloomington, IN, Solution Tree Press.

Shirky, C. (2008). *Here Comes Everybody: The power of organizing without organizations.* New York, Penguin Press.

Stephens, D. J. (2013). *Hacking your Education: Ditch the lectures, save tens of thousands, and learn more than your peers ever will.* London, Perigee Books.

Thomas, D. and J. S. Brown (2011). *A New Culture of Learning: Cultivating the imagination for a world of constant change.* Lexington, KY, CreateSpace.

1 Understanding creativity

KEY QUESTIONS

- Why is it so difficult to define creativity?
- What is the orthodox view of creativity in UK education?
- How do teachers understand creativity?
- What is social about creativity and why does it matter?

Introduction

In this chapter, we turn our attention to questions of creativity in education. We begin with some examples of how creativity has been considered within higher education, before moving our thoughts to the context of formal schooling. But before we do that, a Reflective Task!

REFLECTIVE TASK

Spend a few moments thinking about how you would define 'creativity'. What are the key words or phrases you would include in your definition?

In 2002, the Imaginative Curriculum Network[1] was established by the Higher Education Academy as home to a community of people interested in developing the creativity of students in higher education. The impulse behind the network was a recognition that UK universities were not valuing creativity in ways that would guarantee its place in the curriculum. Proponents of creativity argued that this would be costly in a world where increased complexity and speed of change demands those human qualities and dispositions that are not covered by curricula which emphasise skills and outcomes. Very similar arguments have ranged in recent discussions about the role and purpose of a National Curriculum within the school context. However, what exactly was it that people were not valuing? What is meant when we talk of creativity?

Norman Jackson from the Network began asking these questions of academics working in British universities. He discovered that a number of ideas were commonly associated with creativity (Jackson 2003). Over the past year we have informally replicated Jackson's work by talking to teachers and colleagues with whom we work, and have come up with very similar findings. Below is Jackson's list of common ideas together with glosses informed by our own conversations and email exchanges with teachers and lecturers.

Originality

Creativity is about adding something that wasn't there before. Some people are seen as 'original', they don't repeat what has already been said but are able to add something new. Originality is something that some people, special people, possess.

Being imaginative

Imagination plays a crucial part in people's conception of creativity. Again, this is understood as a disposition: some people have a great imagination and can often think beyond the immediately obvious into a realm that is new. Others can't; their imagination, like a pipeline to the source of creativity, is easily blocked.

Exploring for the purpose of discovery

A creative mind is a curious mind, constantly pushing the boundaries and taking risks in order to experience new things. When those new things can't be discovered, they have to be created. It takes great energy and confidence to explore, to discover. Often the institutions in which we work make it difficult to explore and can seem threatened by it, preferring instead to manage exploration that ultimately maintains the status quo.

Doing/producing new things

Creative people invent stuff – things and ideas, but these are special people, with special powers. Invention just comes to you, at moments you might least suspect. If, though, it doesn't, you can't chase it.

Doing or producing things no-one has ever done before

Creative people generate innovative ideas. Innovation is the current buzzword with which activities are associated to make them sound valuable.

Doing or producing things that have been done before, but differently

It is much easier to think outside the box when you step outside the box. Cross-disciplinary work, the fertilisation of one idea in a particular area by ideas that have been generated in a completely different area, can provide new pathways for solving problems.

Communication

Unless an idea is shared, the creative process is somehow incomplete.

It is instructive that these understandings of creativity include such common elements. How do Jackson's thoughts about creativity relate to your response to the opening Reflective Task?

We do seem to have a shared frame through which we view the idea of creativity. However, this is just the *idea* of creativity. As Jackson points out, this list needs to be seen and evaluated in the context of actual practice. Therefore he turns to studies (McGoldrick 2002; Oliver 2002) that asked academics in the United Kingdom a more specific question: 'What does being creative mean when you design a course?' Interestingly, context seems to have little impact on their answers. Very similar associations are made, with the addition of promoting the idea of 'graduateness' (defined as the ability to make connections between what has been learnt and how to transfer that knowledge to other situations), and being able to produce a narrative of the work which complies with the institutional requirements of course design. The latter clearly expresses that moment of 'creative compromise' where fiercely held personal ideas meet institutional regulations and expectations.

Jackson and his colleagues in the Imaginative Curriculum Network discovered that UK academics and students, whilst sharing some ways of thinking about creativity, found it difficult to specify a conclusive single definition of the concept. Again, this reflects research reported in a number of reviews of creativity published in the past fifteen years (Boden 1991; Loveless 2002; Craft 2003). There is an assumption that creativity involves novelty and originality; usefulness and value, but synthesising those terms into a convincing definition has proved elusive. We really are not sure what is meant by creativity. Is it the 'product', some tangible thing that is new and useful? Alternatively, is it the 'invention' and the process leading up to the invention (Runco 2007: 385) that we should think of as creativity? Or is it some kind of cognitive process that has intrinsic value?

Is all creativity the same? Researchers of creativity often make a distinction between a kind of everyday creativity which allows us to improvise our lives in the midst of constant change, and 'extraordinary creativity' which is 'the sort of publicly acclaimed creativity which changes knowledge and/or our perspective on the world' (Craft 2003: 114). A similar idea is often expressed by the terms 'eminent-level creativity', those discoveries that are particularly important for society, and 'non-eminent-level creativity', our innate ability to adapt to different circumstances that has given us evolutionary advantage (Richards 1999). Is there a sense of elitism creeping in here? The mundane, evolutionary survival behaviour disappearing into the background of the everyday, whilst the extraordinary creativity, the person with unusual, special talents, emerges as the real creative? Could it also be that this idea is reinforced by associating the real creative with the arts, rather than science or technology?

These questions and the tensions they produce are not new. In 1999, a report called *All Our Futures*, published by the UK National Advisory Committee on Creative and Cultural Education, argued the case for a more 'democratic', inclusive understanding of creativity, 'one which recognises the potential for creative achievement in all fields of human activity; and the capacity for such achievements in the many and not the few' (NACCCE 1999: 31). The report emerged against a background of economic stagnation in the UK and the fear that economic progress and prosperity would be thwarted unless the potential of every young person could be harnessed. Its solution was to make recommendations for a national strategy, both in content and pedagogy, addressed to the government, educators, parents ... 'everyone' (the report was, after all, called *All Our Futures*) for creative and cultural education.

The definition of creativity contained within the report is succinct:

> Our starting point is to recognise four characteristics of creative processes. First, they always involve thinking or behaving imaginatively. Second, overall this imaginative activity is purposeful: that is, it is directed to achieving an objective. Third, these processes must generate something original. Fourth, the outcome must be of value in relation to the objective. We therefore define creativity as imaginative activity fashioned so as to produce outcomes that are both original and of value. (NACCCE 1999: 30)

This definition has become so influential in subsequent educational policy that it has acquired the status of orthodoxy. It might have begun as an indicative, stipulative definition designed, perhaps, to encourage exploration and empirical investigation, but through transformation, repetition and modification it has acquired the status of truth. This is what creativity is; now, how do we go about teaching it? It was used by the QCA's 2004 report *Creativity: Find it, promote it* (QCA 2005), which translated the definition into practice through prescribed activities. The report *Nurturing Creativity in Young People* (Roberts et al. 2006) used it in a policy framework. Ofsted referenced *All Our Futures* in its *Learning: Creative approaches that raise standards* (Ofsted 2010). At least, a discussion of the definition is *de rigeur* in most educational textbooks, and its baseline definition is constantly referred to in designing and assessing curricula and classroom tasks. What began as a stipulative definition has morphed into sets of orthodox principles. As orthodoxy, the definition has become common sense. Although teachers may find it difficult to articulate an abstract definition of creativity, we would argue that it is NACCCE's definition that, implicitly, is used in classrooms when creativity is introduced, discussed and assessed.

However, is it right? Must the product of imaginative activity have an objective? Must it have value? Whose objective? Whose value? Is creativity really about producing something original?

The rest of this chapter makes a case for disturbing the 'common sense' that is expressed in this orthodoxy around creativity. We want to replace the frame we currently use to look at creativity with another, one that will lead us towards a more distributed and socially networked understanding that can, we argue, respond more effectively to the ways we are increasingly living and learning.

Connecting

Instead of trying to define creativity, Steven Johnson, in his book *Where Good Ideas Come From* (Johnson 2010) looks at how we talk about creativity, at the metaphors we commonly use to describe the moment when a great idea emerges. So, we talk of the light-bulb moment, the eureka moment, the flash of inspiration, the epiphany. These ways of talking actually frame what we see and understand. They privilege a particular view of creativity. This is the view that an idea is a single thing, which occurs at a single moment. According to Johnson, the metaphor is unhelpful if not completely misleading. He suggests that ideas are in fact networks. At a primary, neurological level, an idea starts out as new connections between neurons in the brain. As an organ built on the basis of its ability to constantly create new connections between neurons, this is simply what the brain was built to do. If that is how new ideas happen, then the most important question becomes how to get yourself into an environment where new connections between neurons in the brain are most likely to be formed. A metaphor, which, he argues, more closely encapsulates this process is the swarm.

We are familiar with the idea of swarming – that collective behaviour that leads to the uncanny coordination of collective action when, for example, a flock of starlings turn and twist over the landscape, or when the queen bee leaves the colony with a group of worker bees to create a new home and more nectar stores. Johnson argues that this metaphor is useful in helping us to understand the process of creativity, which thrives not in flocks or colonies but in networks. It is in networks where the connections between ideas and people can thrive, and sometimes produce a great idea. The problem is that when we explain where a great idea came from, instead of describing the uncanny coordination of collective action, we tend to revert to the ingrained metaphor and talk about the flash of inspiration. Therefore, after the seminar where, through debate, discussion, argument and deliberation, the great idea emerged, we might very well recount it as 'that moment when Dave had a flash of inspiration and came up with that great idea'. It is difficult to think of creativity without that metaphor.

Johnson argues that not only is the metaphor misleading, history also shows how wrong the frame produced from it is. From examples as diverse as Tim Berners-Lee's idea for the World Wide Web to Darwin's idea of natural selection, Johnson shows how the idea is very often manifested as a hunch. This hunch, however, is not a flash, but more like a lingering, slow-burning feeling or intuition that can live in the back of the mind for decades before it becomes accessible and useful. That is because good ideas arise from the collision of smaller hunches that eventually connect together to become something bigger than themselves. It is a rule well known in Hollywood: you do not have a really good idea until you combine two little ideas (Tharp and Reiter 2006: 97). Of course, you need an environment with physical spaces for those collisions to take place. In the Enlightenment, the collisions took place in the coffee houses of London. Ideas were discussed and debated, leading to innovations in science, business and politics. The cultural innovation of the 1920s, during the period we refer to as modernism, took place when writers, poets and artists of every type hung out in the same cafes in Paris. These were inter-disciplinary or even anti-disciplinary spaces, public spaces where a real mix of people discussed ideas, foregrounding some and forcing others into the background to wait, perhaps until the time was ripe for them. These were the social networks of their day. Support networks amongst friends, yes, but also networks that encouraged connections between divergent people and ideas. We will discuss this in greater detail in Chapter 3, but here it is key for Johnson's argument that what he calls 'liquid networks' allow for the movement of information from one context to another completely different context: between friends, but more importantly between friends of friends' friends.

Another key idea for Johnson's theory is Stuart Kauffman's concept of the 'adjacent possible', which Kauffman uses to explain how such powerful biological innovations as sight and flight came into being. Johnson describes the concept by analogy:

> think of [adjacent possibility] as a house that magically expands with each door you open. You begin in a room with four doors, each leading to a new room you haven't visited yet. These rooms are the adjacent possible. However, once you open one of those doors and stroll into that room, three new doors appear, each leading to a brand new room that you could not have reached from your original starting point. Keep opening doors and eventually you have built a palace. (Johnson 2010: 31)

At any point in time, only certain next steps are possible. YouTube could not be invented until broadband and cheap video cameras had been invented. The concept is equally applicable to innovations in science, technology and culture. The central core of the theory of the adjacent possible is that people arrive at the best new ideas when they combine prior (adjacent) ideas in new ways. Whilst most combinations fail, a few succeed impressively: 'good ideas are not conjured out of thin air; they are built out of a collection of existing parts, the composition of which expands and occasionally contracts over time' (Johnson 2010: 35).

Importantly, adjacent possibilities are most evident and most easily explored through liquid networks. The more nodes in the network, the greater the movement of divergent information through the network, the greater the opportunity for building ideas and things from adjacent possibilities.

What Johnson offers in *Where Good Ideas Come From* is a view of creativity that rejects the idea of the solitary genius, whose ideas emerge in flashes of inspiration. Instead, he argues that creativity is resolutely social, dynamic and material. A creative idea may have its beginnings in a hunch, but for that small hunch to emerge into a great idea, it needs cross-fertilising in physical environments where subtle forms of cooperation replace uninhibited competition. All ideas, even the most radical, he argues, build on the ideas and recycled bits and pieces of older inventions. As he says, aphoristically, 'chance favours the connected mind' (Johnson 2010: 22).

PRACTICAL TASK

Johnson talks of the popularity and importance of the commonplace book during the Enlightenment (Johnson 2010: 84), full of notes, quotations and other ideas that allowed for reflection and revelation through re-reading. Try keeping a commonplace book of your own. Add quotations, thoughts, ideas and re-read your entries after a week. Look for adjacent possibilities: have you noticed any ideas combining with others in ways that you had not noticed while you were writing in it? Have you expanded your next move?

Liquid networks are clearly important as a store of divergent ideas and things that can be plundered. How could you build such a network in your school? What tools might you use? How would you encourage divergence? How much of the work you do is available for others to build on?

Resist the temptation to lean on technology. Johnson reminds us that 'the most productive tool for generating good ideas remains the circle of humans at a table, talking shop' (Johnson 2010: 61). How might you create stronger face-to-face networks in your professional life?

These ideas have some powerful resonances with the basic educational activities and processes that all teachers deal with day-by-day. In the next part of this chapter, we take one of the activities – reading – and see how the ideas around networks and their connections can begin to transform something as 'simple' as reading a book.

Connected reading

For years, we have annotated books. From notes scribbled in the margins to post-it notes stuck to pages, we've also copied chunks of books into essays and letters sent to friends, sharing the ideas of other writers with other readers. In a sense, we were liberating the book-bound text from its covers and enabling it to live in miscellaneous excerpts, serving our own purposes, with our own readers/network. Isn't this one of the *raisons d'être* of books in the first place? They want to be annotated, underlined, dog-eared, cross-referenced and talked about.

The e-book has enabled that inherent quality of books to grow to a new level by allowing readers to highlight individual passages and then extract those highlights and read them again in another, new text. We can annotate our highlights by making notes, and read those together with the passages they offer commentary on. By turning a digital switch, we can also share those highlights with other readers and read passages that have been highlighted by other readers. As a teacher, you can share annotations and notes with your students as you are reading a particular book, helping them through difficult passages and suggesting supplementary readings as you go along. This is just the beginning of the kinds of activities that e-ink is allowing through various devices. As yet, the sharing is not very sophisticated. It is either public or private. I can't specify a particular reading group with whom to share my highlights, notes and annotations. But these fine-grained choices, together with greater flexibility around highlighting and linking text across books and different media, are emerging and allowing me to be more specific about what, and with whom, I share.

When texts are moved from the paper page to the networked screen, reading itself becomes more social. One of the problems with the Kindle and other e-readers is that they tend to exist in silos: as devices, they do not talk to each other very well. On the web, however, that limitation is removed and, together with the rise in tablet computers, we are seeing some important innovations that harness the social potential of online reading.

These ideas of creativity and connectivity can be found in many educational projects around the globe. If digital technologies and ubiquitous networks are changing the ways in which we learn and acquire knowledge, what are the effects on the ways in which we read? What affordances does networked reading offer for the teacher? How do networks enable reading to be a more social activity?

CASE STUDY: COLLECTIVE AND CONNECTED READING

Let's pick an amazing book and have our students connect and share our thoughts.[2]

The idea is a simple one: to get a whole city to read the same book at the same time. It began to take shape in Seattle in the late 1990s, when the city was invited to read *The Sweet Hereafter* by Russell Banks, and since then many cities have run programmes where, at a particular time in the year, one book is chosen to be read by the whole community. In Brighton, City Reads[3] is one example among many where collective reading is building up communities of readers young and old, exploring books through meetings, lectures, discussions and author events.

The internet is heavily involved in this renaissance of social reading, and it is beginning to expand the scope of school reading out into the farther reaches of the connections we can make across distances and time zones.

Instead of city-wide reading, some teachers have been generating global reading initiatives that lever the power of the internet to connect readers across continents. A great example of this is the Global Read Aloud Program started by Pernille Ripp in 2010.[4] Pernille is a primary school teacher in the USA who decided to expand her primary class reading sessions and book projects to include the whole world. The idea and its organisation is simple: for a six-week period, each class that is participating in the programme reads a chapter of the chosen book aloud. For each week's chapter, the class also completes a project and shares it with classrooms doing the same throughout the world. Various ways of sharing can be used. Some classes write Tweets on post-it notes that are then shared on Twitter by the teacher, with a hashtag common to all the classes in the programme. Classes can use a dedicated Wiki or blogs to share their work. Classes talk to each other using Skype or Google Hangouts. Even those classrooms that lack technology and may not be connected to the internet can participate: there are many postal-partners, who quickly develop into reading-pen-pals.

What is particularly instructive about this project is that it began with a simple idea. That idea was posted on a blog with a couple of suggestions as to how a global reading community could be created. That post was then Tweeted and re-Tweeted, and almost immediately the network of teachers connected to Pernille were asking where they could sign up. She set up a new blog, globalreadaloud.com, and a Google form to collect information about who was interested. The first Read Aloud programme ran in 2010 with sixty teachers and 300 students. They chose to read *The Little Prince*, and each week Skyped, drew and wrote their responses to chapter tasks as one big community. In the second year, exactly the same premise and ground rules led to 3000 children being connected. By 2013, thirty countries on six different continents were bringing together over 144,000 students.[5] It's becoming very much a global project, but without the kinds of global efforts that you might have associated with such projects before we had the digital network and the tools to leverage its affordances. Once those tools are in place, it simply grows organically. Here's what one teacher, Matt Renwick, said of his experiences with Global Read Aloud in 2012:

> The Global Read Aloud was an excellent learning opportunity. It enhanced our read aloud experience and modeled for students how to draw upon a variety of resources and experiences in order to become more knowledgeable and responsible citizens. The technology tools were great, but they only facilitated what was more important: The connections we made with other people from around the world. Thanks go to Mrs. Ripp for making this happen.[6]

This year's Global Read Aloud gives you the opportunity to connect your class together with classrooms throughout the world. You may or may not take up that opportunity. More important, though, is the paradigm shift that Global Read Aloud represents, and which you could reproduce and build on in a variety of ways:

- Creating a year-wide reading hashtag to share responses to class readers amongst different classes;

- Starting a reading blog where your school's teachers share what they're reading. You could interview teachers about the books they've enjoyed and share those interviews on the blog. Connect your blog to others;

- Working in partnership with other schools in your area, expand the possibilities for connection and collaboration through Skype exchanges or a shared Wiki.

What Global Read Aloud shows is that such efforts will grow. The passion for reading, and a desire to share the responses we have to that reading, can now be harnessed to connect us all beyond our geographical and cultural homes.

The tools of connected reading

The Global Read Aloud project shows clearly that one of the key directions of innovation has been to try to enable readers of any text online to leave annotations and share them with others. Diigo and CommentPress are two very different platforms that are representative of this kind of collaboration. Like Delicious, Diigo (an abbreviation of 'Digest of internet information, groups and other stuff') is a social bookmarking site that allows users to bookmark and tag web pages.[7] However, it also allows users to highlight any parts of those pages and attach sticky notes to them. These annotations can be public or private, shared with everyone or with a specific group or class. With group sticky notes, members of the group can interact and discuss important points right on the web page. Teachers can incorporate prompts and support directly on the text they want the group to work on.

CommentPress is a Wordpress plugin and theme that allows readers to comment in the margins of a text.[8] Blog readers have always had the option of commenting on a particular blog post. However, CommentPress allows a more finely grained commentary and discussion, either on fixed documents or on blog posts. As teachers, we have used CommentPress to develop reading skills by annotating texts ourselves with prompts and questions to guide reading and generate discussion.

Both Diigo and CommentPress have been around for some time, but new platforms are emerging all the time. Rap Genius is a site where 'artists and their fans explore lyrics interactively via line-by-line annotations they can read, create and edit as part of a worldwide knowledge project'.[9] Initially it focussed on rap lyrics, but by 2014 it had expanded to housing the collected works of Shakespeare and Jane Austen, TV and film scripts, the poetry of T. S. Eliot, and news items from current affairs. Each text has become annotated by thousands of readers who, in doing so, have provided detailed exegesis around extensive discussion.

Subtext[10] is both a web and free iPad app for collaborative reading which, once signed into, allows teachers to bring in reading content (web pages, pdf files, books, open-source material via Google Books) to share with a class. You can then embed questions, prompts, polls, video and links directly into the text. Students can work collaboratively on a text in class in real time, or elsewhere asynchronously. Students can also work on text they themselves choose in ways that lead to peer-supported learning through annotations. It does seem that we are in the midst of a major involvement by educational publishing in the e-reader and digital reading market. Ponder[11] is another platform that has been gaining popularity in the past two years. It is a browser add-on that allows students to create and share micro-responses on any web page. Those micro-responses consist of highlights (words, phrases or sentences that provoke a response); sentiments (students choose from a range of reactions); and themes (set up by the teacher to scaffold skills or content for the students). These responses are then pulled together as a class feed that aggregates all the activity on the text by the group. Finally, increasing numbers of platforms and apps are generating data about the ways students share their understanding of, and responses to, the readings they engage with. Curriculet,[12] for example, uses an algorithm that allows teachers to scan student data in order to establish how long students engaged with the text, when they completed the reading, how many questions they used to scaffold their understanding, and other information about the reading experience.

This is only a very brief introduction into some of the tools and ways in which networked knowledge is changing how we read. The paper-bound books we read today are the results of numerous innovations in design and technology over the past 250 years. Reading a parchment is a different experience from reading a paperback. Reading in a networked world through digital screens can also be a very different experience. But is it a better educational experience? That is a question of design, and within a learning context the possibility of connecting people through the texts they engage with is a real positive. Building reading groups across classes, schools, even countries; enhancing book discovery and recommendations through a personal network; building social and intellectual credibility for the process of reading – all these components become more possible through social reading in networks.

Stealing

As we are exploring throughout this chapter, being connected is a central tenet of being creative. We are not creative in a vacuum. Creativity is not an abstract disposition that is mysteriously bestowed on a few extraordinary people. One key thinker who has explored this idea in significant detail is the writer, cartoonist and designer Austin Kleon. His book *Steal Like an Artist* (Kleon 2012) begins with a quote from T. S. Eliot which summarises its central idea: 'Immature poets imitate; mature poets steal; bad poets deface what they take, and good poets make it into something better, or at least something different' (Kleon 2012: 4). In literature, then, a writer transforms a word or phrase used by another writer into something that becomes his or her own. This is accomplished by providing a new use, a new meaning or new context. Sometimes what is written is better than what it was stolen from. Sometimes it is interestingly different. What it is not, is original.

Kleon adds to our understanding of this chapter's key theme because he looks directly at what we might call the 'sector divide' (the idea that there are particular sectors, such as the arts, where the real, extraordinary creative minds work) in so many discussions of creativity and says, very simply, there is 'nothing new under the sun' (Ecclesiastes 1: 9). Rather than feeling depressed by such sacrilege, Kleon embraces and celebrates the idea. In order to do something new, we do not have to sit around trying to be original, we can instead embrace what influences us and develop the ideas we steal honestly. This solution is not an easy one. The process might seem easy, but the resistance we meet in embracing it can be fierce.

Kleon tells a story about the composer Stravinsky to make the point. Stravinsky is best known for his ballet score *The Rite of Spring* that scandalised audiences at its premier in 1913. Some years later, he wrote another score for ballet. To compose it, he took scores from older, less famous composers and started editing them as if they were his own. He re-jigged bass lines, modified harmonies and orchestration, and tinkered with rhythm (Ross 2007). When the piece, *Pulcinella*, was performed, Stravinsky was 'attacked for being a pasticheur, chided for composing "simple" music, blamed for deserting "modernism", accused of renouncing his "true Russian heritage"'. People who had never heard of, or cared about, the originals cried 'sacrilege': 'The classics are ours. Leave the classics alone.' Stravinsky's answer to those critics? 'You "respect", but I love' (Nichols 2002: 141). The latter phrase has become well known and is often quoted. But was it really a phrase that Stravinsky came up with? Perhaps not. Scott Messing (1988) claims that the remark was made by a member of the audience in a performance of *Pulcinella* and, through a process of Chinese whispers, made it to Stravinsky's lips. The quest for the 'original', even here, remains elusive. However, does it matter?

Kleon thinks that it does, but not in the manner of proving who the originator was in a game of one-upmanship. In 2010, Kleon published a book of poems called *Newspaper Blackout*. The poems were written by taking pages from newspapers, and boxing words and phrases on them that jumped out. Those words and phrases were then joined together into a combination and the words that were not needed were blacked out using a marker pen (Kleon 2014a).

Although Kleon initially thought he was copying the idea from redacted documents coming out of government departments, he soon began to realise how unoriginal he was, and that there was a rich history of working with newspapers in the way he was doing. He searched for the genealogy of the idea and traced it to an artist in the United Kingdom, Tom Phillips, whose work *A Humument* is based on the pages of a book over which Phillips draws, leaving some of the text to create a new story.[13] Phillips himself, he soon realised, was influenced by William S. Burroughs, the US beat poet who used a method he called 'cut ups' to re-arrange words, phrases and paragraphs to create new works. Burroughs was influenced by his friend Brion Gysin, who cut up and re-arranged newspaper sections at random in a piece called *Minutes to Go* in 1959.[14] That idea goes back to Tristan Tzara, a French surrealist who created a poem at an event in Paris in the 1920s by pulling words torn from a newspaper out of a hat. Finally (but is it ever finally?), the impulse to reassemble newspapers can be traced to an eighteenth-century Scottish wine merchant and diplomat, Caleb Whitefoord, who used a novel way of reading newspapers he called 'cross-reading'. He read across the columns of articles on the page, producing new meanings from unplanned juxtaposition.[15]

Kleon's *Newspaper Blackout* and the various influences that led to it over the centuries are reminders both of the concrete ways in which stuff is made through dismantling, copying, tinkering and reassembly, and of the importance of influence.

Let's look at influence first. In *Steal Like an Artist*, Kleon advises his reader to build his or her own genealogy of influence, person by person. That means getting to know the artist or role model well. Reading everything they have written. Then to follow three people by whom they were influenced, and do the same for each of those. That means being endlessly curious and digging ever deeper as you uncover more and more. The idea is that you can build a tree of influence around a particular activity so strong that ultimately you can become your own branch of that tree. Of course, the ideas and the influences have to be good. You have to select carefully those ideas and people that will influence you, because ultimately you will be a product of those ideas and influences. As Kleon says: 'You have a mother and you have a father. You possess features from both of them, but the sum of you is bigger than their parts. You're a remix of your mom and dad and all your ancestors'(Kleon 2010: 6). Influence works in the same way. We all have to build worlds of influence so that we can produce good work.

In the Introduction, we talked about spoon making in Edale. One of the things we noted was the way in which copying spoons was an integral part of learning how to carve them. It is far from a mindless activity. Copying carving positions, handgrips and axe cuts is a vital part of learning the craft. Knowing who to copy is clearly key, but the carving gurus are evident and the crowds quickly gather round them, watching eagerly as they carve. Copying spoon styles is not only about learning which shapes necessitate which knife cuts, but also about developing an individual style. Copy one carver and everyone will reference that carver when they see your spoon ('Nice. Looks just like a Jarrod spoon'), but if you copy fifty carvers in carving one spoon, the response is more likely to be 'Nice, I can see you're developing your own style'. It's very similar to the adage: good copying is scholarship, bad copying is plagiarism. Kleon is trying to develop a manifesto of creativity by acknowledging and working through the idea that all art is theft. He suggests that we will need to cultivate certain human qualities for the creative life. Things such as kindness, curiosity, 'productive procrastination', a willingness to look stupid and a hobbyist mind-set. He exhorts us to 'write the book you want to read', 'do good work and share it with people' as well as 'be boring (it's the only way to get work done)'. In addition, if he wants us to steal, he wants us to do so in a way that guarantees our interaction with the ideas that shape us and respect some important precepts. He illustrates those in a characteristically informal sketch (Kleon 2014b).

Kleon's work is fresh and stimulating, and as I was reading *Steal Like an Artist* I annotated it with copious notes, some of which have been reassembled here. In a sense, I made my own unique copy that includes reactions and references to other writers who have lead me through the paths that Kleon outlines. Why not make your own notes in the margins of this book (assuming it's your copy and not the library's)? If you have a blog, include those notes in a post to share with others. Alternatively, write snippets from your notes on a postcard and pin it to a noticeboard; see who comments and what they say. Join in the dialogue.

PRACTICAL TASK

Here are three short tasks to help explore the key messages of Kleon's, and our, work on 'stealing'.

1 Begin to create your own tree of influence in teaching and learning. Who has inspired you? Who inspired them? (Remember, for every one person who inspired you, try to find out three people who inspired them.) Make notes. Identify ideas that were shared by the branches in your tree. Learn about those ideas. Dig into the detail. Be curious.

2 Here's an exercise that is similar to Stravinsky's editing of the manuscripts of past masters. Join a Twitter chat for teachers (you can find a useful list of such chats at creativeeducation.com).[16] Many of these chats are held at specific times of the week and the transcripts of the chat sessions are then archived. Choose a session that you are particularly passionate about and edit the transcript into a document that you can share with others who you encourage to continue the process. Check Kleon's list. How good was your theft?

3 Kleon is keen on sharing. His new book is called *Show Your Work* (Kleon 2014c) and outlines ten ways in which you can share your creativity. However, importantly, what Kleon is keen on is sharing the process of creating something, sharing the dots that you connected in order to write or do what you did. Think of a good lesson that you have taught. Chart the dots you connected in order to produce that lesson. Give the dots to someone else. Ask them to create a lesson from them. What can you learn from their attempt?

Combining and remixing

> I believe that creativity is a combinatorial force – it happens when existing
> pieces of knowledge, ideas, memories and inspiration coalesce into incredible
> new formations. And in order to make a concept (or product, or idea, or
> argument) fully congeal in your head, you have to first understand all the
> little pieces that surround it – pieces across art, design, music, science,
> technology, philosophy, cultural history, politics, psychology, sociology,
> ecology, anthropology, you-name-itology. Pieces that build your mental pool
> of resources, which you then combine into original concepts that are stronger,
> smarter, richer, deeper and more impactful – the foundation of creativity.
> (Popova 2014)

Austin Kleon's world of creativity is a world of interacting with our influences, of building on what has gone before, transforming and remixing it to make something that speaks with a new voice. His own book is, of course, a remix of elements read before in works such as Rilke's *Letters to a Young Poet* (2011), Amenoff's *Letters to a Young Artist* (2006), Twyla Tharp's *The Creative Habit* (Tharp and Reiter 2006), Bayles and Orland's *Art and Fear* (2012) and David Shields' *Reality Hunger* (2010).

This notion of the remix actually has its origins in Jamaica where, during the late 1960s and early 1970s, music producers such as Lee 'Scratch' Perry played stripped-down instrumental versions of popular reggae songs. Initially these producers just removed the voice tracks, but later they started dropping new tracks and production effects into the mix. Later that remix culture moved to New York and morphed into hip-hop music where live musical collages, similar to the literary cut ups of William Burroughs, were made through cutting and scratching on turntables and mixing decks. When digital sampling emerged in the 1990s, new music began to be assembled not by emulating older music, but from their actual sounds. Art of Noise were one of the first groups to create music entirely from the samples of others.

Remix, then, very simply, is the idea that someone makes something by combining cultural resources together. Someone else then comes along and remixes that something that was made by someone else by adding new things to it. And so on. Kirby Ferguson, in an excellent documentary on remix culture, shows how music and films are developed through remixing. Not surprisingly his documentary is called *Everything is a Remix*[17], and from this perspective not only is culture a remix, but knowledge, politics, science and technology are all remixes too. Remix is how things get made.

Harvard law professor Lawrence Lessig argues that there are two goods that remixes make: one is the good of the community and the other is education (Lessig 2008). He illustrates this idea of the community good by looking at the culture and practices of anime music videos (AMV). These are videos created by remixing images from anime cartoons with a music track or the track from a movie trailer.

Many of the producers of these videos are young people sitting at home recording anime cartoons from the TV, capturing images, re-editing them and synchronising them to new soundtracks. The results are often shared online at animemusicvideo. org. Whilst AMV uses cultural content that began in Japanese media, the community involved in its production knows no geographical boundaries. The connections that are made between the cultural resources remixed, the producers and the audiences are not limited to towns and streets. The web allows groups to form and communities of interest to develop very, very easily. The groups that form in the AMV community include many young people who just want to learn. They remix in order to develop the digital skills to make sophisticated media pieces. They show off. They teach each other. They become talented producers who are able to remix works that are very beautiful. Lessig tells the story of one parent whose son failed to get into university, but when he showed the admission team his AMV creations they accepted him immediately.

When you watch young people using these technologies – collecting stuff, editing and mixing it, transforming it into something new that expresses something about themselves in that moment – you begin to see how they engage in active, creative remixing of the culture that is around them. Through these tools, we also glimpse how different that cultural world is from the one it has succeeded. Lessig calls the twentieth-century world of media a 'read-only' world. Media was something produced by the professional few and consumed by everyone else through an ever-improving series of appliances: phonographs, broadcast radio and television, video, DVD, HD ... and latterly the internet. This world was very different from the world it replaced.[18] Before the professionalisation of the media and its dissemination for consumption, people did make their own. Media were 'read–write', whether in work songs or oral story telling. Now, in the twenty-first century, we are actually returning to that culture. It is the culture of the remix, of the amateur making of stuff sitting beside its professional counterpart, cross-fertilising and cross-contaminating with it in a spirit of productive use or, as Axel Bruns famously calls it 'produsage' (Bruns 2008).

There are many examples of remixing as a classroom strategy[19] to explore ways of writing using new multi-media tools for making meaning. One that Lessig recounts is a project that ran in a Los Angeles school in a poor area of the city. The school was failing on all traditional measures of success. But when two teachers in the school ran a Friday afternoon class which gave the students the opportunity to use film to express something they knew about and were deeply connected to – gun violence – their problem was not so much getting the students to participate, but actually getting them to stop and go home. These students were working harder than in any other class – to express themselves. The teacher described the class as using whatever 'free stuff' they could find on the web, together with simple digital tools to enable them to mix image, sound and text (Lessig 2004: 39). Not only did the students produce remixes that communicated their meanings about gun violence, that few people living outside the context in which they lived would otherwise understand, they did so in a language and form that was congruent with the experiences of their lives.

However, there is a problem. Twenty-first-century practices of creativity are sitting inside twentieth-century laws: a lot of this creativity is technically illegal. Our laws do not recognise the derivative nature of creativity. This is one of the reasons why there is such a disconnect between how young people create stuff out of school and what they do inside. It is worth teasing out the detail a little here because it will put into context some of the tensions that currently exist in our world of media use. The problem comes down to the belief, which has grown up in the past 250 years, that ideas are property and that laws are needed to protect that property from being stolen.

Two articles of law protect ideas as property: patents (which deal with inventions) and copyright (which deals with media). Here we focus on copyright, because it is the most relevant. Many of the most obvious uses of, say, a book are unregulated by copyright laws. Reading it, sharing it, giving it away as a present, reselling it, annotating it – all these uses do not infringe copyright laws. Making a small number of photocopies and distributing those to a group of students, or quoting from the book in a review article, are also unregulated by the law as they are considered as 'fair use', that is, a public good. However, if you republish that book, copyright laws regulate your activity. The reason for this is that original creations cannot compete with copies. It may take me weeks to write a book and there is a cost associated with its production. It takes a lot less to republish it, and the cost is obviously reduced. Copyright was originally intended to protect this difference. It protects and encourages the creation of new ideas by providing a period of exclusivity, the time frame where nobody can copy your work. After the period ends, the work enters the public domain and can be copied and freely built upon.

However, this example of the book is completely overturned when it becomes a digital artefact distributed over the internet. The nature of the digital network is that every use of a digital artefact produces a copy. This means that my sharing the e-book, giving it as a gift and reselling it are governed by copyright. If a publisher wants to impose a condition that I cannot read an e-book or film more than once in a month, they can easily do so. Software can be embedded that denies access when those conditions are infringed. Although fair use is often invoked for educational use, the category is very approximately delineated[20] and can be offputting to a teacher. Not so for young people, who will continue to use technology to 'crack' the digital rights management technology that has been layered into content in an attempt to control free cultural activity and place it into copyright jurisdiction. This is their language and they will appropriate it.

With the arrival of the read–write culture, networks of amateur production have developed in all kinds of spheres, from cartoons to gymnastic tutorials. The communities that emerge are producing things, but these things are not considered in monetary terms. They do not fall so easily into the equation that great ideas = property = financial gain. The millions of uploaded videos, music, blog posts and discussion board comments are not taking part in a commercial economy and do not look for the kinds of protection afforded that economy. We will see how this sharing economy has grown in Chapter 4.

What is important here is that accompanying this growth in content has been the development of a series of technologies that enable the creators of content to mark it with the freedoms that they want their work to carry. This tells anyone who wants to use or remix the work about the conditions under which they are permitted to do so. This is the principle around Creative Commons, a not-for-profit organisation that issues licences (Creative Commons licences) free of charge to the public in order to expand the range of work available for others to build upon and share.[21] When you make something, you can visit the Creative Commons website and choose a licence to apply to your work. You can choose amongst licences that permit or constrain commercial uses of your work, or permit or constrain modifications to the work and the conditions under which those who modify the work are entitled to release that work to the public. You can, for example, have a licence that permits modification and sharing only if the subsequent work carries the same licence as yours. These licences exist as machine-readable legal expressions. This means you can use search engines to gather content based on the permissions to remix and share. By 2011 there were, at a very conservative estimate, over 400 million works released under Creative Commons licencing. Not only can Creative Commons allay the fears of many in education about the risks of piracy, they offer a door into a vital exploration of how culture can best be created. They become another tool to enable, in Kleon's words, good stealing.

It is easy to criticise remix culture. Its practice can focus on the minutiae of digital editing – hours and hours of copying and pasting, clipping and cropping. It can be a mindless appropriation involving little critical thinking, whilst celebrating celebrity. It may involve shallow, superficial engagement with a narrow range of content. It can wilfully ignore ethical issues. Of course, the same can be true of formal writing. Just as there is good writing and bad writing, there is good remix and bad remix. There is remixes that enables the practice of multi-media skills and multi-modal expression. The communities of interest it can establish offer the possibilities of immersive participation and develop key cultural identities. The best remix raises critical questions about media, copyright, fair use and plagiarism.

Beyond the good versus the bad, however, what remix has shown us here is how creativity is about connecting the cultural dots. Whether in an email, a photograph, a film, a chapter of a book, or a remix of George Bush and Tony Blair lip-syncing to *Endless Love*,[22] we are constantly joining the dots together. Remixing is a folk art, but the techniques are the same ones used at any level of creation: 'collect, copy, transform and combine'.

Connected writing

Earlier in this chapter, we explored how concepts relating to creativity and connection impacted on processes of reading together. In a similar way, the discussion about creativity, connection, combining and remixing has an interesting analogue to another key educational activity that all students undertake every day: writing.

This book, like all books, has been written within a network of collaborators, some more visible than others, and some more explicit contributors than others. As we are increasingly seeing in organisations, businesses, schools and universities, collaboration is becoming the way in which things get done. The reason, as Douglas Thomas and John Seely Brown identify, is that 'almost every difficult issue we face today is a collective, rather than a personal problem' (Thomas and Brown 2011).

One of the most difficult forms of collaboration is writing. Writing collaboratively, from passing bits of paper between two or more people in a room to working across physical distance and time zones in an online virtual office, demands a different way of thinking; thinking that understands the importance of networks. Network writing re-defines the process of writing. It is no longer a question of squeezing inspiration out of a single brain; it is about connecting distributed knowledge and understanding and making collective sense.

The idea of emailing Microsoft Word drafts back and forward between multiple collaborators is a difficult way of collaborating. It may be useful during a period of final editing (if the process of tracking changes is followed rigorously by everyone), but for actual collaborative writing it can be difficult to use.

Fortunately, there are an increasing number of tools now available on the web that enable collaborative writing. What is interesting about these developments is less the final product (collaboration is about the ways in which tools are used, not the tools themselves) than the process of learning about collaboration that emerges as you play with them. Here are four tools that we think you should look at, play with and incorporate into student writing activities.

Google Docs (docs.google.com)

This is a constantly evolving ecosystem of writing, commenting, sharing and editing privileges for documents that live in a shared Cloud. You can use a Google document for writing synchronously, with multiple writers contributing at the same time on the same document; or for writing asynchronously, where a document is written at different times by different authors. In the asynchronous form, writing the document can be integrated with video conference support (through Google Hangouts) or simple online chat. This kind of working can result in the document being co-written through a process of conversation. At best, it is social writing.

Piratepad (www.piratepad.ca)

In Piratepad, anyone can create a new collaborative document (a 'pad') with its own URL. Anyone who knows that URL can access the pad, edit it, and contribute to chat sessions associated with it. Security-by-obscurity can be augmented by password-protected pads. Each collaborator is identified by both name and colour. You can collaborate in synchronous or asynchronous mode and see previous versions as they evolved through a time slider. It can be embedded in another platform, for example a class blog, which means you and a number of students could collaborate in real time, with an audience watching you write.

Piratepad works really well in brainstorming sessions and for concentrated intensive collaborative writing. The slider feature means that you can see the final text unfold during the composition stages – a great way to show students how important iterative editing is. It can also be a powerful formative assessment tool. We rarely get it right first time, and this shows how and why edits are made and the effect they have. One session that we ran with Piratepad showed how the theory of the adjacent possible (see Chapter 2) works with language; how one word/phrase suggests one but not another possibility and how we build our prose in that way.

Piratepad is a hosted instance of the original open source programme Etherpad. Etherpad could easily be installed on a school server, allowing for greater privacy and data management.

Draft (draftin.com)

This tool has a simple, very clean-looking writing interface for working with editors or getting feedback from peers on a piece of writing-in-progress. There are few distractions in the interface; the focus is on the writing. If (like us) you can get caught up in over-editing at too early a stage in the writing process, you can use 'Hemingway mode', which disables the 'delete' button. That means you are forced to move forward towards completing a section before you start editing. Again, using this with students will practically and graphically introduce what editing is and how best to practise it.

Penflip (penflip.com)

Penflip is a collaborative writing tool modelled on the revision-control system used by software teams on GitHub (a collaborative software development platform). The idea of the tool is that every collaborator on a drafted document makes a master copy that they revise and improve on. That document is then offered back to the owner of the first draft, who can decide whether to merge the two documents together to make a third or to stick with the first. Again, this can be used in the classroom as a way of looking at editing criteria and the decisions we make in deciding whether one version is better than another.

Writing collaboratively is one way of showing how knowledge is distributed and emerges in a network. Clearly there are many options, and which one you might want to choose depends on the purposes of the writing activity that you are planning for your particular students.

Collaborating

So far, our emphasis on creativity as a social process has implied rather than directly explored its collaborative and cooperative nature. We have considered how it impacts upon educational activities such as reading and writing together. Clearly, however, working with others is so often an integral part of the creative process, whether in clusters, networks or communities, that it deserves our attention. Johnson, Kleon, Popova and Lehrer have all recognised the importance of connecting with people in order to develop ideas and build on what has gone before. However, how does this interpersonal process unfold? In *Group Genius* (Sawyer 2007), Keith Sawyer explores the 'moment-to-moment interactional dynamics' of collaboration, adding to the evidence that creativity emerges in collaboration.

Sawyer's earliest research into the creative power of collaboration was sparked by Jazz Freddy, an improvisational theatre company based in Chicago. After watching them, Sawyer wondered: 'How can ten people go on stage and create such a complex and entertaining performance when they have absolutely no idea about what's going to happen?' (Sawyer 2007: 12). He then spent months watching improvisation workshops and performances, making notes, taking videos and talking to the performers. From his analysis of these materials, he identifies some key characteristics of collaborative improvisation:

■ It is highly contingent from moment to moment;

■ There is deliberate ambiguity as the dialogue develops;

■ Each collaborator listens deeply;

■ The meaning of each individual act is emergent;

■ As each actor makes a choice, the possible next choices expand.

One of the interesting elements of these characteristics is the way they explain how conversation works. People in conversation often change direction, pause, and repeat themselves. Some of the most engaging conversations are like dances, each participant leading and being led at the same time, listening carefully for the others' moves. Language itself is deeply embedded in the immediate social context. In the phrase, 'I'm sorry he had to hear that', 'he', and 'that' are ambiguous. Unless you were party to the context and how the phrase emerged from previous utterances, you would not be able to guess what they referred to. However, that ambiguity also allows for a wider array of possibilities for the next utterance. It is not surprising that Sawyer argues that 'constant conversation' is an essential ingredient for creativity.

REFLECTIVE TASK

Think about a lesson that you are going to teach in the next week or so. How might you design it in a way that takes into account the five characteristics of collaborative improvisation and constant conversation listed above? What difference would this make to how you will teach and how your students will learn?

This way of thinking about teaching relies heavily on trust. Those involved in an improvised performance of any kind have to rely heavily on each other in order to work productively. Sawyer's concept of a 'constant communication' has some interesting analogies to your work as a teacher. In the first instance, a good and trusting relationship with your students is paramount. They have to be secure in their knowledge that you are leading them along an appropriate pathway in their learning. You have to be confident that they are committed to coming with you on that journey. The constant conversation that Sawyer's work highlights is crucial to this. It gives you, and your students, the freedom to talk deeply about the context within which learning takes place, and how the contingencies and ambiguities that are inherent within any learning process can be explored together as new learning emerges.

Secondly, of course, you have relationships with other adults within the school who are also committed to students and their learning. The individual teacher/student relationship that is at the heart of good teaching is shared within a wider school context. The constant communication here will be between you and your colleagues. It needs time and space to develop. This is often difficult in a busy school environment. However, discussions about individual students and their learning are vital in ensuring that each student fulfils their potential as a result of the school's provision. This form of collegial conversation is where Sawyer's work moves next.

Sawyer's aim in *Group Genius* was not only to analyse the nature of improvisation and what it can teach us about creativity. He also wanted his ideas to have an influence in organisations where innovation is increasingly seen as vital to survival. Collaboration is not a twenty-minute brainstorming session or a period of mind mapping. It is a constant conversation where many ideas are explored, where time is devoted to the exploration, and where failure is expected as a normal part of the process. For organisations this needs to happen both internally, where colleagues work together in a culture of conversation, and also externally: organisations need to move into collaborative webs where the conversations can spark new ideas across traditional boundaries. This model of innovative organisation is a corrective to the assumption we saw at the beginning of this chapter – that creativity is the privilege of the solitary genius. Within the corporate domain it is often expressed as the 'great man' theory of creativity. People such as Steve Jobs, Anita Roddick and Bill Gates are accorded almost mythical powers of divergent thinking, spontaneity, novel behaviour and intrinsic motivation to succeed. Sawyer shows us that it is the collaborative webs that an organisation makes within and beyond its boundaries, allowing constant conversation to take place, that ultimately shape how creative it is likely to be. In Chapter 3 we look the importance of such webs, and in Chapter 5 at the ways in which constant conversation of the type Sawyer promotes might be developed in the classroom.

Summary

We started this chapter by looking at the knotty issue of definitions of creativity. We saw how so many educational researchers are interested in unlocking the processes and products of creativity in order to better prepare students for a world where creativity is seen as such an important quality. We have looked outside the world of education at some recent thinking about creativity to stimulate your curiosity and suggest ways that you might imagine the classroom focussed on learning creatively.

Let us now look at an initiative that has integrated many of the elements of creativity that we have been looking at into one educational platform. MIT's free Scratch media creation/remixing/programming platform is named after the idea of disk jockeys 'scratching' records to create new remixes of old songs, as we saw in the section 'Combining and remixing'. Scratch is a desktop or online platform that allows amateur users to combine images, music and sound with programming code and publish their projects to the Scratch website. Since launching in 2007 (not by chance was Keith Sawyer on the advisory board), that website has become an online community often dubbed the 'YouTube of interactive media'.

By July 2014, nearly four million users had created accounts on the system and more than six million projects had been shared.[24] The projects range from video games, interactive newsletters and animations to birthday cards, interactive tutorials and chemistry simulations. Users self-report their ages as between eight and seventeen years old, though many adults also participate. Forty percent of users self-report as female. The goal of Scratch was 'not to prepare people for careers as professional programmers but to nurture a new generation of creative, systematic thinkers comfortable using programming to express their ideas' (Resnick 2008: 19). It was to replace the idea that the web was a place to consume through browsing, clicking and chatting, with simple tools that could create complex media productions:

'There is a buzz in the room when the kids get going on Scratch projects', says Karen Randall, a teacher at the Expo Elementary School. 'Students set design goals for their projects and problem-solve to fix program bugs. They collaborate, cooperate, co-teach. They appreciate the power that Scratch gives them to create their own versions of games and animations.' (Resnick 2008: 21)

Figure 1.1 Screenshot of doglover579 Scratch project page[23]

Scratch uses a drag-and-drop modular system to build generative projects like combining Lego blocks. Once a project is completed and uploaded to the community, any registered user can view it, comment on it, vote for it, or download it back into the interface, modify the scripts and remix it. All projects shared on the site are covered by Creative Commons licences. In remixing Scratch projects, users are encouraged to import media from around the web to incorporate into new projects. What the platform is implicitly arguing for is for the advancement of 'fair use', that rather muddy concept used to avoid breaches of copyright. What it is shouting out is that such use of media is absolutely fair and, more than that, is integral to the learning of a new generation of young people. It is an important stand for such a formal educational platform to take, and one that could have major implications for online creativity in the future.

What then do students learn when they use Scratch? What does this platform have to do with our journey through creativity as a social phenomenon?

■ Scratch extends what children seem to grasp in primary school: that the best ideas come from interacting with your environment (people and things) and sharing what you learn;

■ Scratch allows its users to see how a culture is built from the ground up. This is the creativity that Austin Kleon and Keith Sawyer both refer to. Downloading a bit of culture, tinkering with it, transforming it and uploading it so that others may enjoy it or use it as the basis for their own subsequent ideas;

■ Students using Scratch soon learn that their ideas are dependent on the ideas of others. Collaboratively they can build stuff that is new and then new again, and then new again;

■ Scratch introduces the idea of 'computational thinking', the idea that 'if you can understand how computers think and how humans can talk to them in a language the machines understand, you can imagine a project that a computer could do, and discuss it in a way that will make sense to an actual programmer' (Tasneem 2014). This is the kind of thinking that leads to articulating new problems rather than always attempting to solve existing problems. This is a key idea in Johnson's notion of creativity;

■ Finally, by downloading, remixing, uploading, discussing, liking, sharing and generally hanging out, scratchers are participating in a community fuelled by a common interest and driven by a continual curiosity and need to make better stuff.

In *A New Culture of Learning*, Douglas Thomas and John Seely Brown talk about Scratch and about nine-year-old Sam's experience of using it.

> When we asked Sam what it meant to be a good member of the Scratch community, he didn't say building games or posting animations. He said, to 'not be mean' in your comments. In other words, he got the coding, but the real thing he was learning was how to work with other people effectively. When we asked him what he looked for in other people's programs, he said, 'something really cool you would never know yourself'. So he was learning how to learn from others. (Thomas and Brown 2011: 23)

His first lesson of creativity.

Let's end this chapter by sharing a little hunch that we have been developing as we have reviewed these ideas about creativity. Could it be that this current obsession with creativity, especially in educational and corporate contexts, is a distraction from a more difficult but perhaps more interesting question? If we watch very carefully how young people innovate, we see how they quickly create peer groups to identify with, learn with, cooperate with and compete with in order to push the activity they engage in to the limits of the possible. Consider, for example, the extreme sport of free running. Free runners work together. Once a new move is created, it is not patented or copyrighted. Instead, it's posted on YouTube and within forty-eight hours it's been copied around the planet by thousands of enthusiasts. They have to be enthusiasts to be bothered. Enthusiasm is a key quality that enables learning. As is curiosity. Free runners will not only study free running to improve. They will use whatever they can. They will look at skateboarding, gymnastics, capoeira, martial arts, mountain biking, any adjacent activity that will expand the possible. However, vitally, that 'possible' has to be imagined. Without imagination, any of the problem-solving creativity that we have been discussing in this chapter cannot grow.

Notes

1 imaginativecurriculumnetwork.pbworks.com
2 theinteractiveteacher.com/pernille-ripp
3 cityreads.co.uk/about/collected-works-cic
4 www.globalreadaloud.com
5 theinteractiveteacher.com/pernille-ripp
6 readingbyexample.com/2012/11/28/the-global-read-aloud
7 www.diigo.com
8 wordpress.org/plugins/commentpress-core
9 news.genius.com/Genius-genius-for-iphone-is-here-annotated
10 www.renaissance.com/products/subtext
11 www.ponder.co
12 www.curriculet.com
13 www.humument.com
14 briongysin.com/?p=742
15 intercapillaryspace.blogspot.co.uk/2006/05/caleb-whitefoord-cross-reading.html
16 www.creativeeducation.co.uk/blog/index.php/2010/12/top-twitter-hashtags-for-uk-teachers
17 everythingisaremix.info/watch-the-series
18 'The twentieth century was the first time in the history of human culture when popular culture had become professionalised, and when the people had been taught to defer to the professional.' (Lessig 2008)
19 digitalis.nwp.org/search?search=remix
20 'How much of a work can I use under fair dealing?
   There is no simple formula or percentage that can be applied. You may have seen figures like 'up to 10%' or 'no more than 400 words' quoted in some publications, but such figures are at best a rough guide and can be misleading. What is acceptable will vary from one work to another.
   In cases that have come to trial what is clear is that it is the perceived importance of the copied content rather than simply the quantity that counts. Judges hearing such cases often have to make an objective decision on whether the use is justified or excessive.' (UKCS 2009)
21 creativecommons.org
22 www.youtube.com/watch?v=UpRhkz-QoRQ
23 Image licensed under the Creative Commons Attribution-ShareAlike license. Scratch is developed by the Lifelong Kindergarten Group at the MIT Media Lab. scratch.mit.edu/projects/14663895
24 scratch.mit.edu/statistics

References

Amenoff, G. (2006). *Letters to a Young Artist*. New York, Darte Publishing.
Bayles, D. and Orland, T. (2012). *Art & Fear: Observations on the perils (and rewards) of artmaking*. Santa Barbara, CA, Capra Press
Boden, M. A. (1991). *The Creative Mind: Myths & mechanisms*. New York, Basic Books.
Bruns, A. (2008). *Blogs, Wikipedia, Second Life, and Beyond: From production to produsage*. New York, Peter Lang.

Craft, A. (2003). 'The limits to creativity in education: dilemmas for the educator'. *British Journal of Educational Studies* 51 (2), 113–127.

Jackson, N. (2003). 'Creativity in Higher Education', York, Higher Education Academy. 78.158.56.101/archive/palatine/files/1015.pdf [last accessed 2/8/14].

Johnson, S. (2010). *Where Good Ideas Come From: The natural history of innovation.* New York, Riverhead Books.

Kleon, A. (2010). *Newspaper Blackout.* New York, Harper Perennial.

Kleon, A. (2012). *Steal Like an Artist: 10 things nobody told you about being creative.* New York, Workman.

Kleon, A. (2014a). 'Neighbours'. www.flickr.com/photos/deathtogutenberg/14407547896 [last accessed 4/11/14].

Kleon, A. (2014b). 'Steal like an artist – 'good theft vs. bad theft'. www.flickr.com/photos/deathtogutenberg/6784163064/ [last accessed 4/11/14].

Kleon, A. (2014c). *Show Your Work! 10 ways to share your creativity and get discovered.* New York, Workman.

Lehrer, J. (2012). *Imagine: How creativity works.* Boston, MA: Houghton Mifflin Harcourt.

Lessig, L. (2004). *Free Culture: How big media uses technology and the law to lock down culture and control creativity.* New York, Penguin.

Lessig, L. (2008). *Remix: Making art and commerce thrive in the hybrid economy.* New York, Penguin.

Loveless, A. (2002). *Literature Review in Creativity, New Technologies and Learning,* Futurelab Research report 4. Bristol, NESTA, Futurelab. telearn.archives-ouvertes.fr/hal-00190439

McGoldrick, C. (2002). 'Creativity and curriculum design: what academics think'. Paper for the Learning and Teaching Support Network (LTSN) Generic Centre, York, UK.

Messing, S. (1988). *Neoclassicism in Music: From the genesis of the concept through the Schoenberg/Stravinsky polemic.* Ann Arbor, MI, UMI Research Press.

NACCCE (1999). *All our Futures: Creativity, culture and education,* Report to the Secretary of State for Education and Employment [and] the Secretary of State for Culture, Media and Sport. London, National Advisory Committee on Creative and Cultural Education.

Nichols, R. (2002). *The Harlequin Years: Music in Paris, 1917–1929.* Berkeley, CA, University of California Press.

Ofsted (2010). *Learning: Creative approaches that raise standards.* London, Ofsted.

Oliver, M. (2002). 'Creativity and the curriculum design process: a case study'. Paper for the Learning and Teaching Support Network (LTSN) Generic Centre, UK.

Phillips, T. (2012). *A Humument: A Treated Victorian Novel.* London, Thames & Hudson.

Popova, M. (2014). 'Mission'. www.brainpickings.org/index.php/mission/ [last accessed 2/8/14].

QCA (2005). *Creativity: Find it, promote it.* London, Qualifications and Curriculum Authority.

Richards, R. (1999). 'Everyday creativity', in *Encyclopedia of Creativity*, M. A. Runco and S. Pritzker, eds. San Diego, CA, Academic Press, 683–688.

Rilke, R. M. L. C. (2011). *Letters to a Young Poet & The Letter from the Young Worker.* London, Penguin.

Roberts, P. et al. (2006). *Nurturing Creativity in Young People: A report to government to inform future policy.* London, Department for Culture, Media and Sport.

Ross, A. (2007). *The Rest is Noise: Listening to the twentieth century.* New York, Farrar, Straus and Giroux.

Runco, M. A. (2007). 'Creativity theories and themes: research, development, and practice'. site.ebrary.com/id/10158387 [last accessed 2/8/14].

Sawyer, R. K. (2007). *Group Genius: The creative power of collaboration*. New York, Basic Books.

Shields, D. (2010). *Reality Hunger: A manifesto*. New York, Alfred A. Knopf.

Tasneem, R. (2014). 'We can code it: why computer literacy is key to winning the 21st century', *Mother Jones*, No. 6. www.motherjones.com/media/2014/06/computer-science-programming-code-diversity-sexism-education [last accessed 1/8/14].

Tharp, T. and Reiter, M. (2006). *The Creative Habit: Learn it and use it for life: a practical guide*. New York, Simon & Schuster.

Thomas, D. and Brown, J. S. (2011). *A New Culture of Learning: Cultivating the imagination for a world of constant change*. Lexington, KY, CreateSpace.

UKCS (2009) *Using the Work of Others*, Fact Sheet P-27. Didcot, UK, UK Copyright Service. www.copyrightservice.co.uk/copyright/p27_work_of_others

2 Networks, creativity and learning

KEY QUESTIONS

- What are networks, and why is it a surprise to discover how small our worlds really are?
- How are our lives shaped by networks?
- How is learning shaped by networks and the connections we are able to make in and between them?
- Is there any theory that might help us make sense of learning in a network society?

What are networks?

Networks have become a vital part of our lives in the past few years with the spread of digital technologies, and particularly social media. We use them to find jobs, friends and even life-long partners. We mine them for information to help us fix the car or plan a lesson. But what are networks? What do we know about them? This chapter introduces some of the key moments in the story of networks to suggest that knowing a little more about this story can furnish us with a lot of understanding that will improve our lives in and out of the classroom.

Simply put, networks are things that tie other things together. Our planet itself is a network of inter-connected fault lines and weather patterns. Networks of roots and capillaries transport food to plants, enabling them to live and grow. Cities are tied together through road networks routed through junctions and intersections. Humans form networks in order to tie people together. We tie together because we are social and that's how we nourish our humanity. It's not just spies or old boys who join together in networks. Bonds between families, communities, villages and nations are created and nurtured through networks. In fact, the writing of this book, our checking of emails, receiving of phone calls and bills paid all make use of networks. Networks remind us of the responsibility of the individual to the community, and even to the propagation of the species. No-thing and no-one operates in isolation. We can be autonomous, in the sense of acting alone, but because of the ties that bind we are always providing or curtailing support for those to whom we are connected. When the individual thrives, the community thrives. When communities lose support through a withdrawing of connections, those communities wither.

Harry Beck: mapping the network

One of the most important principles of networks is the idea that the connections between the elements of a system are more important than their specific positions in space and the relative distances between them. Here's a story that graphically illustrates that principle.

The London Underground has been running under the streets of the capital since January 1863, when 30,000 people travelled on the Metropolitan Line on its first day of operation. Now upwards of a billion people travel on the system every year. For tourists visiting London, a trip on the Tube is as important as a visit to Buckingham Palace, seeing the Houses of Parliament and shopping in Oxford Street. Curiously, the most popular journey on the Underground with tourists, between Leicester Square and Covent Garden, is also the shortest. It's 260 metres and takes only about twenty seconds.

But perhaps even more iconic for visitors to London is the map of the Underground developed by Harry Beck in 1931. Beck was an engineering draughtsman who worked for the London Underground Signals Office. Every day he worked with maps of the Underground which, although geographically accurate, were a mess of curving lines and station points with above-ground streets superimposed over the whole thing. When reduced to its pocket version, the map was at best confusing. Beck's passion for simplifying complexity led him to develop a radically new map which sacrificed geographical accuracy for schematic simplicity. He replaced the curving lines with straight horizontals and verticals. Instead of using scale to represent distance, he placed stations at equal distance from each other and removed the overlay of above-ground streets. As Claire Dobbin says, 'the genius of Beck was that he realised that the exact geographical or topological cores of the line is not necessarily essential to the Underground passenger' (Dobbin and London Transport Museum 2012).

The reason why Beck's map was so successful was that he recognised that, underground, the sequence of stations was more important than geographic accuracy. The connections between stations and the interchange options from individual stations are more important than geographic distance. This is vital in the understanding and use of networks. In the language of network science: topology is more important than metrics. Not only was the new map much easier to use, it changed the way people move in and around London and even, it can be argued, helped create the suburbs of the capital by making them appear closer to the centre, thereby encouraging people to move there.

Harry Beck was paid ten guineas (£700 in today's money) for a map that has become iconic for London and an influence on transit system maps throughout the world. Whilst the topography of the world's major cities may have grown increasingly chaotic, the principles for representing transport networks have remained largely the same since 1931. These principles have stimulated others to use Beck's method to schematically represent other systems where the connections between points are more important than the points themselves. So in 2006 Dorian Lynskey used the Underground map to chart the branches, connections and interchanges in 100 years of music (Lynskey 2014). Lynskey said of his project:

> The elegance and logic of Harry Beck's design ... seems to spark other connections and appeal to the brain's innate desire for patterning and structure. (Lynskey 2014)

PRACTICAL TASK

Teaching is a complex network of people, subjects, communities and much more besides. Beck's work on the design of a new map for the London Underground helps us see how key components of a network can be re-imagined or re-conceptualised. The impact of this alternative visualisation and the re-positioning of key components can have a profound impact on human behaviour.

Revisit the previous Reflective Task, which asks you to consider the key components of the network that surrounds your teaching. If you haven't done already, sketch out the key components of your teaching network on a piece of paper. Can you begin to identify core sets of themes that could begin to be grouped together? Can you begin the process of simplifying the themes and re-positioning them to reprioritise the way in which they are connected? For example, is it possible to identify the key components that relate to:

- Your subject and how it is taught;
- Your students and their lives both within and beyond the school boundary;
- People who have been, or are, influential to your thinking about education;
- Key organisations with which you engage regularly;
- Processes of professional development or performance management;
- Your local area and how it implicates and informs your work in your community.

As you consider the construction of this personal network, can you begin to trace how information or other 'stuff' begins to flow around it? Who are the key figures or organisations within it? How do key parts in the network exert power and influence over other elements within it? Are there marginalised, fragile or unsupported elements within the network?

These types of questions, and others that we explore below, will begin to help you gain a detailed understanding of the powers, influences and personalities that exist in the network within which your work as a teacher is located. We return to these ideas in future Reflective and Practical Tasks.

Jacob Moreno: a person's psycho-social self is built in networks

What is interesting about network approaches to complex systems is that they focus on the interactions between phenomena in a system, not on the individual components of that system. Representations of systems such as electricity grids, flight routes and ecosystems often make use of graphs to show the connections between phenomena (or nodes). Whilst these can be somewhat abstract, the advantage of using them is that we can focus on the general patterns between phenomena without getting bogged down in the performance of the particular. This means that the connections between seemingly disparate, disconnected events or phenomena can be seen more easily. This is what Beck achieved, and why his map has been so influential in helping millions of people find their ways around the different areas of metropolitan London.

Humans have always lived in social networks mediated by forms of communication, and the endeavour to understand such systems is not new. In the years just after the first world war, Jacob Moreno, psychotherapist and early explorer of the application of network theory to social relationships (he coined a word, 'sociometry' to describe the method), began working at the displaced persons camp in Mitterndorf in Austria. There were tensions in the camp because of the differing social, linguistic, religious and cultural characteristics of the refugees, many coming from the region of the South Tyrol which had been occupied by Italy at the end of the war. The barracks where the refugees were housed took no notice of these differences. Moreno did. He looked at the choices that people made as they gathered together. Where they sat. Who they sat with. Who was central to the group and who was peripheral. On the basis of his observations, he drew sociograms (what we now more commonly refer to as 'social graphs') showing the connections. From these graphs, plans were made to re-group the refugees. Once re-grouped, stress and tension was reduced in the camp and relations between the refugees improved.

Perhaps Moreno's best known use of sociometry was his long-range study at the New York State Training School for Girls in New York between 1932 and 1938. This was another marginalised group characterised as 'delinquent'. Some of the girls absconded from the school and were labelled as runaways. Moreno hypothesised that the runaways were motivated not necessarily by their individual attitudes or the conditions in which they lived, but by their positions in the underlying structure of the group – their sociogram. Again he observed the girls, individually and in their various groupings, and set tasks so that he could establish not only the current network/structure between the girls (one that resulted in runaways), but also so that he could change the dynamics/connections in ways that would reduce the problems and the number of girls who did run away (Marineau 1989). Moreno's work attracted a great deal of attention at the time, with *The New York Times* carrying an article in 1933 entitled 'Emotions mapped by new geography' and including one of Moreno's sociometric graphs.

The kinds of exercises that Moreno carried out in the school in New York are easily repeatable, and give a graphic sense of how sociometry and network theory work.

PRACTICAL TASK

Find a suitable class and ask them the question: 'Which member of this class would you most trust to keep a secret? Move around the room and choose one person by placing your right hand on their shoulder. You cannot not choose.'

When the class has completed the task, you can sketch the connections on an interactive whiteboard creating, as you do so, the social graph based on this one criterion – trustworthiness. You may notice clusters, chains and even big gaps. Save the image.

Change the choice to be made. 'Which member of the class would you choose if you wanted to generate creative ideas for a class project?' Notice the differences and compare the image with the one saved from the previous question. The group could then talk about how the graphs reflect real life, and how informal organisation often sits a little hidden from the formal organisation, though imperceptibly influencing it.

There are also various online versions of this exercise that you can try. Sometics[1] allows you to create a sociogram online using a variety of criteria and group sizes.

Moreno believed that large-scale social phenomena such as the state or the economy are constructed from the small-scale configurations formed by people's patterns of friendships, likes and dislikes (Moreno 1941). Our own experience as educators suggests that his central insight informs how we work with students to create groups, and how groups can be organised into communities. It's in the patterns of interaction where the richest information about the informal and formal organisation lies (Caldarelli 2012).

These concepts are easily observable in any classroom. Next time you ask your students to undertake an activity through a piece of group work, make a deliberate decision to step back from the hurly-burly of the classroom and watch the interactions between students in light of the above comments. If the students have been given the freedom to form their own groups for the task, who do they choose to work with? If you have chosen the groups yourself, what criteria have you chosen, and are these criteria shared with the students? How do they feel about them, and how do the relationships within the group develop because of them? Do they have the desired effect?

But these considerations are just the first level in developing your understanding of the network. As Caldarelli teaches us (ibid), it is in the patterns of interaction where the richest elements of both the formal and informal dimensions of organisation can be found. For us, this is where our focus as teachers should be principally fixed. It is where evidence of our students' learning is located.

The human interactions that occur in a group context, like the dynamics of a class or within a specific group-work exercise of the type imagined above, are the first tier of the educational network. During the previous Practical Task, other tiers will no doubt have begun to emerge in your thinking. These tiers relate to a significantly more substantial network that will embrace:

- The notion of individual academic subjects and their specific histories and cultures;

- The curriculum frameworks that position these subjects in particular ways;

- What is often referred to as the 'hidden' curriculum that is promoted by an institution and how it recognises and promotes particular values within its structures, by who we are, how we act, communicate and work with our peers and our students;

- The local area and its communities, history, geographical features and culture which shape the work of the institutions within it;

- The broader expectations that are placed on the work of schools by politicians, policy-makers, local and national accountability frameworks, and other measures by which your work is assessed and judgements are made.

In Chapter 4 we turn our attention to these in further detail and consider how your work as an individual teacher is implicated by the inter-relationships between these networks.

Kevin Bacon and six degrees of separation

It is not just that connections are the most salient features of networks. It is through connections that we understand how small our world actually is.

The intuitive appeal of finding patterns and joining the dots, which stimulated both Harry Becks and Jacob Moreno, also led three students in the USA to speculate how important the actor Kevin Bacon is in the movie industry. Their hypothesis, brewed up while they watched movies during a snowstorm in Pennsylvania, was that because Kevin Bacon was present in so many movies they had seen, and claimed that he had worked with everyone in Hollywood, then he must be the centre of the industry. To test their hypothesis, they invented a game: name any actor and find a chain of collaboration that links that actor to Kevin Bacon. The game spawned a website, 'The Oracle of Bacon',[2] which queries the Internet Movie Database[3] to discover chains of collaboration between two actors. So, what's the shortest path between Elizabeth Taylor and Kevin Bacon? Elizabeth Taylor was in *The White Cliffs of Dover* (1944) with Roddy McDowell, who was in *The Big Picture* (1989) with Kevin Bacon.

The students' idea was based on an urban myth that had been around for a very long time. It's actually traceable to the work of Guglielmo Marconi, known as the inventor of radio who, in his Nobel lecture of 1909, described a system for transmitting and receiving electricity over distance. His wireless telegraphy explored the minimum number of permanent stations and their relative positions able to receive and transmit radio signals across the Atlantic Ocean. It was that speech which inspired celebrated Hungarian author and satirist Frigyes Karinthy's short story *Chains*, published in 1929. The story fictionalises a challenge to find another person to whom the central protagonist could not be connected by no more than five people:

> To demonstrate that people on Earth today are much closer than ever, a member of the group suggested a test. He offered a bet that we could name any person among Earth's one and a half billion inhabitants and through at most five acquaintances, one of which he knew personally, he could link to the chosen one. (Barabási 2002)

The idea that, in a world of now over six billion people, everyone is connected by just a few steps is a tantalising one. That's to say that you know someone, who knows someone, who knows someone, who knows someone, who knows someone, who knows ... me!, or anyone else on the planet.

Almost forty years after *Chains*, Stanley Milgram, an American psychologist, conducted an experiment to test the hypothesis and to discover how many people needed to be known to a person in order to connect two randomly selected individuals. The experiment consisted of sending letters to randomly chosen individuals asking them to forward a package to a 'target', whose address was withheld. Milgram chose two targets: the wife of a divinity student in Sharon, Massachusetts; and a stockbroker in Boston. In order to keep track of the letters, every time someone forwarded the original letter to a friend or acquaintance (someone they knew on first-name terms), they were asked to send a postcard to Milgram. Within a few days, this word-of-mouth-like procedure resulted in the first letter arriving at its destination after passing through only two intermediate links. After a few weeks, almost a third of the letters had arrived at one or other of the targets. None had been posted more than ten times, and the average number of intermediate postings was six. Milgram himself never formulated his results as the 'six degrees of separation'. That was an expression used by John Guare, who used it for the title of his 1991 Broadway play, later turned into a movie starring Will Smith (who was also in *Men in Black* with Rosemary Howard, who was in *R.I.P.D.* with ... Kevin Bacon). Milgram published the results of his study (Travers and Milgram 1969: 119) in *Sociometry*, the journal that was founded by Jacob Moreno. It really does seem to be a small world.

Whilst Milgram's experimental methodology had its flaws (fewer than a third of the sent packages arrived at their target, and though these had passed through an average path length of 5.5, the majority of the packages actually had not arrived anywhere near the original target), he added support to our intuitions that we live in a small, connected world. He speculated that what we mean when we say 'what a small world' is that we live in networks with surprisingly few chains of separation between people, despite the fact that, at the same time, we tend to live in tight groups of close friends. This is worth explaining.

When we talk of small-world networks (and we owe the idea to Milgram), we are talking of networks that display two principal characteristics:

- My connections are likely to be connected to each other;

- The average number of connections (intermediaries) needed to connect any two people across the network (also called the average path length) is relatively short. (We're talking people here to make it easier to grasp, but it could equally well be cells, web links or any other network phenomenon.)

Of course, it remains remarkable that *any* of the packages that Milgram sent arrived at their destination, and so the idea that small-world networks create unique performance benefits for systems became established. More recently, email experiments have confirmed Milgram's findings (Dodds et al. 2003: 67).

Milgram's other important discovery from his experiment was that almost sixty percent of all the transmissions passed through the same four people. Here is the idea of the 'superconnector': we are not all connected to each other, but in fact we can easily find each other, and connect if we do so, through those people who are disproportionally well connected. This also means that if the superconnector disappears, then so do lots of possible connections.

In the 1960s and early 1970s an American sociologist, Mark Granovetter, began to use Milgram's observations to examine how people found jobs in the Boston area of Massachusetts. What he found was that eighty percent of the people he studied did not find a job through a contact with whom they had a close relationship. Instead, they found jobs through friends of these contacts. Granovetter published his results in a book, *Getting a Job* (Granovetter 1974), although his paper 'The strength of weak ties' (Granovetter 1983) has generated more interest, and its title has become something of a mantra in management circles.

REFLECTIVE TASK

Return to the work in the previous Practical Task that helped you map out the network that surrounds your work as a teacher. Can you identify superconnectors within your network, through which many other components pass? How many degrees of separation exist between specific components within your network? What happens if those superconnectors are removed from the network?

The notion of superconnectors is highly relevant for education. Within the broader reach of your network will be powerful agencies such as the Department for Education and Ofsted, for example, whose influence extends to and affects the work of schools, and the teachers within schools, in many different ways. One powerful example of this in recent years relates to the changes in assessment within the new National Curriculum that was introduced in September 2014. This removed the requirement for schools to use levels of attainment in their assessment and accountability processes for the vast majority of subjects. However, these new-found freedoms have not been embraced by schools, many of whom are continuing to use levels of attainment or similar systems to provide the raw 'data' that they think they need to account for their students' progress against national targets.

Whilst the Department for Education has set policy in this area, it is Ofsted that is seen by most schools to be the key regulatory body in this area (a clear example of a superconnector). What Ofsted says it wants to see and how this relates to policy as set by the Department for Education are often at odds, and various degrees of confusion have resulted, leaving many school leaders unhappy about what it is they should or should not be doing.

Also within this educational network are various subject associations who are all fighting for their own views about their subject and how it should be assessed. These organisations have realised that schools have more autonomy in this area and are seeking to promote their own ideas about how assessment should be conducted.

Similarly, commercial companies wanting to make a profit on the sale of assessment materials are entering the fray. These organisations are part of an educational network that, perhaps, has a less charitable and more financial motivation here.

And finally, of course, there are school leaders and teachers who are receiving multiple and often conflicting messages from this extensive network about how assessment should be conducted. This network is a noisy one, with competing voices and challenging ideologies. In our analysis, it is dominated by powerful superconductors who exert influence in unyielding and bureaucratic ways. It is hard for individuals to find their voice in such a network. But one key to their doing so is to understand more clearly how the network works, as well as finding and consolidating their own place within it. Thankfully there are a range of tools and approaches that can help us understand networks more effectively. We turn our attention to these now.

Contemporary network analysis

Whilst the work of Milgram and Granovetter showed the importance of connection, neither showed how those connections work. That had to wait for two figures who have emerged in the past twenty years, together with a new science of networks.

Duncan Watts and Steven Strogatz are two scientists who discovered that the kinds of connections between people that Milgram discovered are also present in all kinds of other areas on our planet: in fact, the idea that we live in a small world seems to be ubiquitous. They started by wondering how patterned behaviour (a group of starlings turning in the sky, fireflies glowing in sync, or the firing of synapses in the brain) is directed when no-one is actually in charge to do the directing. How is synchronous behaviour coordinated when nobody is conducting proceedings? Their hunch, taken from their knowledge of the six degrees of separation, was that nature is itself the behaviour of connections in networks.

In order to explore this hypothesis, they turned to the database used in The Oracle of Bacon and discovered, unsurprisingly, that Kevin Bacon was not the centre of the acting universe, but that the connections between *any* two actors on the database were very small. Just a few hops and you can jump from any one actor to any other. As they expressed this mathematically, they began to realise that they could show the invisible links that demonstrate how a large network can become a small-world network. A highly clustered large network can be transformed into a small-world network by introducing a relatively small number of random distant links as seen in Figures 2.1 and 2.2.

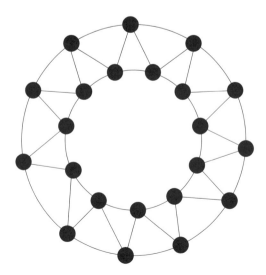

Figure 2.1 Regular network

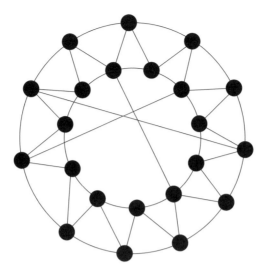

Figure 2.2 Small-world network

Just like the principles used by Harry Beck in representing the Underground schematically, Watts and Strogatz showed us a new perspective on the world, where distance becomes less important than connection.

However, Watts and Strogatz missed something important in their data that would corroborate the second of Milgram's findings. When network scientist Albert-László Barabási looked at the Internet Movie Database, he noticed that whilst there were many actors who had only a few links to other actors, a small number of actors had many links to others. These were the superconnectors, the hubs through which the connections pass. When he continued his analysis on larger networks, including links on the world wide web, he noticed the same small-world patterns emerging. From every single 'page' on the world wide web you can navigate to any other in nineteen clicks or fewer. Search engines, web indexes and aggregates are superconnectors that allow users to move from one area of the web to another. These nodes serve as highly connected hubs. What this means, amongst other things, is that no matter how large the web grows, the same inter-connectedness, the same small-world theory, will apply.

Why is an understanding of networks important? Illustrative stories

Analysing networks is not for the faint-hearted. Because the recent work in network analysis has universal ambitions, it can be full of fine-grained advanced mathematics that deals with vast arrays of data. It is that universality, however, that makes the theory so interesting, important and useful for us as educators. Before we look at how it can be harnessed in understanding teaching and learning in the digital age, let's look at four examples of how network analysis is being employed in other fields.

Terrorist networks

Shortly after the September 11 attacks on the twin towers in New York, Valdis Krebs, a management consultant interested in organisational networks, published a paper in the online journal *First Monday* entitled 'Uncloaking terrorist networks' (Krebs 2002). In it he mapped the organisational network behind the hijacking of the planes from data publicly released in major newspapers such as *The New York Times*, *The Wall Street Journal*, *The Washington Post* and the *Los Angeles Times*. Krebs was able to identify two characteristics of the hijackers' network which enabled it to keep hidden and difficult to identify: it was neither highly centralised nor highly connected. One node could have been eliminated without threat to the network, and the possibility that information could escape from the network was very small. These characteristics, however, did not make the network weak:

> In a normal social network, strong ties reveal the cluster of network players – it is easy to see who is in the group and who is not. In a covert network, because of their low frequency of activation, strong ties may appear to be weak ties. The less active the network, the more difficult it is to discover. Yet, the covert network has a goal to accomplish. Network members must balance the need for secrecy and stealth with the need for frequent and intense task-based communication [...] The covert network must be active at times – it has goals to accomplish. It is during these periods of activity, and increased connectedness, that they may be most vulnerable to discovery. (Krebs 2002)

It also quickly became apparent that the superconnector in the network was Mohammed Atta. He was the closest to the centre of the network, had the most connections and recorded the highest level of activity in the network (Krebs 2002). The metrics support the conclusion that Mohammed Atta was, in fact, the ringleader of the hijackers' group.

Krebs' study was retroactive: he used network analysis to explain how a covert network could organise the attack on the twin towers. The same techniques have been used for understanding the structure of terrorist and criminal networks throughout the world (Sparrow 1991), and would later be used to capture Saddam Hussein in 2003 (Wilson 2010). Indeed, network theory is now an important component in military and police training throughout the world.

Social networks

Although networks can be constituted formally in order to achieve specific objectives (as we've just seen in the analysis of the attack on the twin towers), social connections that we may not even be aware of can influence every aspect of our lives – from who we choose to marry, to decisions about how much we eat. This is the central idea of a book called *Connected: The surprising power of our social networks and how they shape our lives*, which attracted a great deal of interest when it was first published in 2009 (Christakis and Fowler 2010).

The ties that connect networks of people together can enable the propagation of anything that flows across them, including religious ideologies, sexually transmitted diseases and clothing fashions. We both shape our social network (I decide who I befriend, whose friendship I nurture, and which connections I make or break), and also are shaped by it. So, if I have ten friends, who each have ten friends, who in turn have ten friends, I have a much denser friendship network that if I am friends with ten people who are each themselves friendless. There is a much greater potential influence on my life, directly and indirectly, from the people who can influence me, or who influence others who influence me. Of course, there is a natural decay in the level of influence the farther away I am from the source. Christakis and Fowler have calculated that this is generally three degrees: in other words, my actions influence my friend's friend's friend, but no further.

Christakis and Fowler used data from the Framingham Heart Study (2014),[4] which has gathered information about the causes of cardiovascular disease in the small town of Framingham, Massachusetts since 1948. Because the study collected data about the friends, relatives, co-workers and neighbours of participants in this close-knit community over time, they were able to map the social network of more than 50,000 connections, including how these connections changed over the years. Having built the map of the social network, they were then able to chart how phenomena spread through it. Their first observation has had far-reaching consequences. The data enabled them to conclude that obesity is contagious – it spreads like an epidemic from a variety of centres in the network to infect the whole.

Of course, there are a number of caveats. The ways in which we now live and work lead to more sedentary lifestyles which, when combined with changes in the type and amount of food we eat, are factors that go some way to explain current levels of obesity. However, our social networks also play their part:

> Networks can magnify whatever they are seeded with, though other external factors are the initial drivers of the obesity epidemic. If something takes root in a networked population, whether a pathogen or a norm about body size, it can spread across social connections, striking ever larger numbers of people. (Christakis and Fowler 2010: 115)

Not only obesity, then, but also smoking, panic and even suicide can spread within social networks. Fortunately, not only pathogens or negative norms such as these are contagious. Positive emotions also spread – the Framingham data showed that being connected to someone who is happy can have an effect on our own happiness, and that this effect increases at a predictable rate according to the degree of connection.

As we have seen, network science has universal ambitions, and Christakis and Fowler want us to reconsider the way human societies work. Instead of framing the study of human nature as being about the individual versus society, or nature versus nurture, or even culture versus cognition, they invite us to consider human nature as human connection: 'I am ... my connections.' By doing so, they are also able to suggest a third way between understanding society as the result of the choices of individuals (methodological individualism) or the result of the actions of groups whose collective identities cause people to act the way they do (methodological holism).

Individualism and holism shed light on the human condition, but they miss something essential. In contrast to these two traditions, the science of social networks offers an entirely new way of understanding human society, because it is about individuals *and* groups and, indeed, how the former become the latter. Inter-connections between people give rise to phenomena that are not present in individuals or reducible to their solitary desires and actions. Culture itself is one such phenomenon. When we lose our connections, we lose everything (ibid: 303).

Uzzi and Spiro musicals

Our third illustration of networks in action comes from the world of musical theatre. An oft-cited study by Brian Uzzi and Jarrett Spiro investigated the links in a small-world network involving artists working in Broadway musicals between 1945 and 1989 (Uzzi 2005). They wanted to find out whether the connections between artists working on musicals influenced whether or not the musicals achieved critical acclaim. Could they ultimately describe and identify an optimum cluster of connections that would be a sure-fire recipe for creative success? The clusters they identified included composers, lyricists, librettists, choreographers, directors and producers: the teams that created the musicals. From a database of 2,092 artists and 474 musicals, and with 500 artists active in an average year, they set about mapping the connections between them.

They discovered that the informal links that existed between artists who had worked on numerous musicals formed a small-world network (clustered teams) where many densely connected small teams were loosely connected to each other. The results don't sound particularly surprising: producers will call directors they know and trust, who will call composers they are familiar with and respect, who will call ... etc. The adage applies: it's less what you know than who you know. However, their method allowed for more finely grained analysis. They were able to measure the density of the connections in the musical community from the database and gave it a number, represented by Q. If Q is high there are multiple connections between teams and the connections are strong: everybody has worked with everybody else and it's a small-world network. If Q is low there are few connections and those connections are weak: the network is more random and unstructured. What Uzi and Spiro discovered was that Q was large in 1945 and was getting larger, hitting its most densely and strongly connected structure in 1947.

However, the musicals in 1947 did not correspond to those with the greatest success. As Q fell, it passed through a 'bliss point' or 'sweet spot' at around 1950. That's when the optimum Q for success was reached, when the teams were neither too insular nor too open. When there is a Q of 2.6 for the network as a whole, musicals have a 2.5 times greater probability of being successful than if Q is at its lowest value of about 1.4. Above 2.6 the advantage diminishes. In other words, too many connections, and the musical is likely to be less successful. Perhaps there is need of another adage: familiarity breeds contempt?

There are many ramifications of Uzi and Spiro's studies, and many management consultants were quick to oversimplify the small-world theory by suggesting that successful collaboration should balance familiarity and strangeness. That may be true, but the small-world finding relates not to teams *per se*, but to teams that emerge from global measures of a networked community. In other words, Uzi and Spiro's research is less about how to construct individual teams to produce optimum products/creativity, and more about what kind of society can optimise everybody's products/creativity.

Facebook

Our final example of networks is perhaps the most famous and will, most probably, be highly familiar to most readers: Facebook. At the end of 2011, Ugander et al. published a network analysis of Facebook. At the time of the study there were 721 million active Facebook users with 69 billion friendship connections amongst them. Two significant findings emerged from the analysis that was conducted.

The first was that fifty percent of people have over 100 friends on Facebook. This may, at first sight, seem low. If you look at your friends on Facebook you probably see that they all have more than 100 friends listed. This is known as the classic paradox of social networks: most people have fewer friends than their friends have. The reason is that people with more friends are more likely to be your friend than those who are unpopular. You may notice the same thing when you go to the beach on holiday. The beach you choose is always more crowded than the average beach – again, the popularity effect. A study by Backstrom (2011) reports that eighty-four percent of Facebook users have friends who list more friends than they do.

The second finding relates to the number of degrees of separation. Milgram's real-world experiment resulted in any one person being no more than six hops away from any other person. With Facebook:

> While 99.6% of all pairs of users are connected by paths with 5 degrees (6 hops), 92% are connected by only four degrees (5 hops). As Facebook has grown over the years, representing an ever larger fraction of the global population, users have become steadily more connected. The average distance in 2008 was 5.28 hops, while now [2011] it is 4.74. (Ugander et al. 2011)

And the connections have become more concentrated: when the analysis is limited to single countries, the world gets even smaller and most pairs of people are separated by only three degrees. You probably do know a friend of a friend of a friend's friend.

Why are networks important for education?

Over the past twenty years, Manuel Castells has chronicled the ways in which the network has replaced the machine as the organising principle and metaphor for understanding society. His basic argument is that whereas the industrial revolution saw the organisation of society as a linear or serial set of relationships, the new age (what Castells calls the information age), with new communication technologies, facilitates different and more complex interactions that are organised by networks. So *informationalism* has replaced *industrialism* as a paradigm, and introduced with it a new social structure, the network society. Schools, teachers and students are all part of this society:

> What is specific to our world is the extension and augmentation of the body and mind of the human subjects in networks of interaction power fed by microelectronics-based, software operated, communication technologies. These technologies are increasingly diffused throughout the entire realm of human activities by growing miniaturisation. They are converging with new genetic engineering technologies, able to reprogram the communication networks of the living matter. It is on this basis that expands a new social structure as the foundation of our society, the network society. (Castells 2004: 7)

Three characteristics of information and communication technologies have driven this change.

The pace and power of technological change

Firstly, not only has the power of these technologies increased in volume, complexity and speed, but there has also been a qualitative expansion: the technological power of networks is now self-generating. When it looks as if capacity is being reached, a new, smaller, faster piece of technology emerges to push the system to even greater speeds. Few people now complain of insufficient bandwidth to harness the power of video conferencing, and an increasing number take advantage of mobile video calling. The fast pace of technological change is something that anyone working within a school over the past five years cannot have failed to notice. The speed of change often causes problems for institutions such as schools that, by nature and perhaps quite rightly, are slow to change. A simple example could be the ways in which mobile phones are appreciated or not appreciated within the school environment. Whilst some schools are quick to adopt this technology and encourage students to use it regularly throughout their schooling, there are other schools where such devices are frowned upon and students are required to turn them off during the school day. It is not that one approach is wrong and another is right. It is just a sign that our schools and other educational institutions often struggle to adapt and accommodate new technologies appropriately.

The creation, manipulation, combination and sharing of digital content

Castell's second characteristic relates to the nature of content within networks and the ease with which it can be manipulated, combined and shared. When we talk of the constituent parts of the web as 'pages', we are using a metaphor to describe the digitised information that is available over the web. That information is connected with hyperlinks, the combination and recombination of which mean that new output is constantly available for sharing and further recombination. So, innovation and sharing are native to the web by nature of its structure and architecture. As we saw in the Introduction, innovation has become the root of economic productivity and cultural creativity in large part because of the affordances of our information and communication technologies. It is also at the root of knowledge generation: the ability to recombine old information into new patterns and test those patterns out is the way that knowledge is produced and, as we argue, how creativity flourishes.

These native affordances of the web challenge our view of knowledge as a fixed commodity that teachers have in their heads, or in a textbook, and 'deliver' to students within formal structures such as a lesson plan, where certain objectives are prioritised (and others, by definition, are diminished). This raises an important question about what counts as knowledge, and whose opinion about what counts is important. Learning what is required to pass an examination is the most basic form of what counts as knowledge; but what a student should receive by way of an 'education' is much more than this. The web problematises all these areas, and the consequences for how education is shaped and delivered in the twenty-first century have yet to be fully appreciated by our education system. We have more to say on this in the following chapters.

The seamless integration of technology

The third characteristic that Castells points to is the flexibility of these technologies which allows them to be integrated seamlessly into such disparate areas as business, health, the military, personal interaction and education. There seems no part of current society that could be immune to digitisation. This flexibility is currently moving towards the personal – individualised, mobile, wireless communication that centres on the person and not the place. According to Castells, this has enormous implications for our understanding of spatial relations. Where we once had information at different places, we now have networks connecting places by information and communication flows.

Instead of talking about the digital divide (between those included in digital networks and those excluded from them), Castells argues that the most important divide in network society is between what he calls 'self-programmable labour and generic labour':

> Self-programmable labour has the autonomous capacity to focus on the goal assigned to it in the process of production, find the relevant information, recombine it into knowledge, using the available knowledge stock, and apply it in the form of tasks oriented towards the goals of the process. (ibid: 26)

This, he maintains, demands the appropriate training, in terms not of skills but of creative capacity – that capacity to search and recombine from the networks in the production of new knowledge and value. In contrast, generic labour is that work which has little value to the system and which is increasingly either replaced by machines or moved to the current lowest-cost production sites. The vast majority of the world's workers are employed in generic labour. The focus of the world's education systems is on 'programmable labour', preparing people for the demands of the network society.

Preparing students for the world of work is only one of the key aims of an education system. However, as with the pace of technological change discussed above, the type and nature of jobs that our students will undertake throughout their working lives are changing rapidly. Jobs that have not yet been created will become the norm for many of our students. Faced with such an uncertain future, it might seem difficult to plan a coherent education programme. This is certainly true if we focus too narrowly on a job-centred agenda for education. However, some more important things remain, in particular the ability to learn.

How do we learn in networks?

Two writers who have been influenced by network theory and the sociology of Castells are George Siemens and Stephen Downes. Over the past ten years they have explored how we might re-fashion learning for the network society. By looking at networks and social learning in networks, they have developed a framework to understand what learning looks like in the twenty-first century. This framework was given the name 'connectivism' by Siemens in a paper published on his blog in 2005. In 'Connectivism: A learning theory for the digital age' he looks at theories of knowledge that pre-date the current informational, internet era:

> Objectivism (similar to behaviorism) states that reality is external and is objective, and knowledge is gained through experiences. Pragmatism (similar to cognitivism) states that reality is interpreted, and knowledge is negotiated

through experience and thinking. Interpretivism (similar to constructivism) states that reality is internal, and knowledge is constructed. (Siemens 2005)

These traditions, he argues, tell us what learning is, and they have been very influential in shaping classroom pedagogy by providing different models of learning that teachers can understand and promote through their pedagogical processes. Although each of these traditions represents complex theories, Siemens points to weaknesses in their explanations of how learning works.

Behaviourism implies a theory of learning where learning is the creation of habitual responses in specific circumstance and in response to particular stimuli. This leads to the idea of operant conditioning, where students are understood to learn because they are presented with rewards. But there is no explanation of how giving someone a reward stimulates learning. There is simply a move to define what the reward is and begin more exploration in that direction.

In cognitivism, learning is described as creating a change in a learner's mental processes (inner mental activities such as thinking, memory, knowing and problem-solving). Teachers employ strategies for learning that focus on developing students' internal cognitive structures through learning particular techniques, procedures and forms of organisation. Famously, cognitivism describes the mind through the metaphor of the 'black box', internal and knowable only through external manifestations.

Constructivism emphasises that knowledge is something that can be created on the basis of current knowledge and experience. Students learn through the experience of discovery. This happens most effectively through hands-on, collaborative projects that focus on problem-solving and build new knowledge from what people already know (through 'scaffolding'). Exactly how the construction occurs is, however, mysterious, and once again posited on the inner workings of the 'black box' of the mind.

Siemens suggests that common to these ways of thinking about knowledge is that 'learning occurs inside a person' (ibid). What they do not include is the learning that takes place outside of people (institutional knowledge, or knowledge stored in organisational repositories), or between people and actively constituted within social connections. As we have seen in this chapter, our understanding of the world is increasingly informed by our understanding of networks, and more and more networks are informing our world. Siemens is suggesting that learning occurs when we embark on the process of connecting to, and feeding information into, a learning community. That community is a node on a network that connects to other nodes in order to share information. The process is cyclical. We connect to the network to share and find new information. Understanding is changed as a result, and that result is once again shared with the community as we look to find new information. Learning is both knowledge consumption and knowledge creation. So, 'the capacity to form connections between sources of information, and thereby create useful information patterns, is required to learn in our knowledge economy' (ibid).

Many websites, discussion fora, books, articles and online courses have been devoted to discussions of connectivism in the past ten years, and those discussions are ongoing (see the References for a flavour of these). However, from our reading of this literature we have distilled the characteristics of this 'new learning theory of the digital age' into three main components.

Diversity

In connectivism, ways of knowing come from the diversity of ideas, facts and opinions that are flowing through our networks at any one moment. This diversity is organised into information sets, like silos or dots, connected together. No single individual can have control over this diversity. Learning becomes a process of connecting the dots. This process occurs most effectively through cooperation and collaboration. Of course, the more diverse the silos and the ties between them (strong and weak), the better and more interesting the connections made.

Sorting, curating and evaluating

The ability to sort and evaluate information in the network becomes a core skill. We have to be able to see the connections between different sources and join the dots. And not just once. Those connections have to be maintained and nurtured in order for continuous learning to take place. These sources or repositories of knowledge may not be limited to humans. Organisational knowledge and the stores of knowledge in databases can communicate with each other by making their own connections. Network knowledge can be independent of, and grow independently from, human knowledge.

Capacity

Our capacity to know is more important than our actual current knowledge (which implies that great effort must be expended in maintaining and improving that capacity). Choosing what to learn becomes as important a decision as the process of learning itself. Because knowledge is provisional (constantly updated and constantly subject to change) it is more important to be connected to the external flows of knowledge in the network than to acquire knowledge as some form of personal ownership or state.

What is important about connectivism (and paradoxically, from two erstwhile educational technologists) is that it is less about technology and more about creating the conditions, spaces and opportunities for knowledge to be created. Those conditions, spaces and opportunities are found in people and the connections between them: in the networks that people create and nurture. It is also a central argument of this book that schools, and your work within a school, can facilitate these processes for your students.

Notice here that the advocates of connectivism do not suggest that a particular body of knowledge (in the form of curriculum content or discrete syllabus) is transferred from teacher to learner. Rather, the theory holds that knowledge is distributed throughout the network, the web, and learning is connecting to that knowledge. The process of connecting need not be structured or controlled through pedagogical processes, nor need it be motivated by rewards or punishment, nor by social engagement. Because knowledge is not a store of pre-existing 'facts', learning could never be about learning how to store and retrieve such 'facts'. It is about creating the conditions whereby a person can become an effective and motivated learner in their own right and rise to the challenge of managing complex and rapidly changing landscapes.

A theory such as connectivism reflects a growing awareness that information and communication technologies are influencing cognition, and that the fundamental skills of learning in an age of such technologies are changing. More important than the passive memorisation of information is the development of skills ('meta-skills') to access and add to information whenever it is required. The imperative to memorise a piece of information, just in case you need that piece of information at some (undisclosed) time in the future, is replaced by those skills needed to access, retrieve and (if necessary) modify that information as and when it is needed. So, 'just-in-case' learning, becomes 'as-and-when' learning.

In our Introduction, we briefly introduced the work of Howard Rheingold – a leading critic, writer and teacher who has thought hard about social and pedagogical implications of using social media in this way. In eight Tweets written in 2011, Rheingold identified a set of key behaviours that we can adopt and expand on here to help you begin the construction of your own approach to learning within a network. The eight 'behaviours' that Rheingold identified in his Tweets were:

- Exploring;
- Searching;
- Following;
- Tuning;
- Feeding;
- Engaging;
- Enquiring;
- Responding.

Whatever tools you decide to utilise within your personal learning network (and more on that in Chapter 4), these behaviours are vital to cultivate. How will they apply to your work as a teacher? We briefly explore each one below in an extended Reflective Task, together with some questions to prompt your own thinking.

Exploring

According to Rheingold, exploration is an invitation to serendipitous encounter. It is important to be open to new ideas about your teaching and give yourself the best opportunity to encounter new ideas and knowledge about how you can teach better. One of the key skills here is being able to recognise the opportunities inherent within your exploration online. Developing that ability to recognise potential and apply it to your own work takes time, but is worth cultivating. Being 'explorative' is one of the key skills of being an effective teacher.

REFLECTIVE QUESTIONS

- How can I be more receptive and open to new ideas about teaching?

- How can my personal learning network help me explore the opportunities inherent within my contact with new teachers, their ideas about teaching and how it can be done differently?

Searching

Searching productively is linked to exploring. As we discuss below, there are a large range of tools available for you to use here. Searching involves finding interesting stuff, but also capturing and curating it sensibly so you can access it when needed. In terms of building a personal learning network, one of your principal aims here is to identify key people and sources of informative, engaging and provocative thinking about teaching that will help you develop your own thinking and pedagogy further.

REFLECTIVE QUESTIONS

- What tools do I use already to help me search for new information or people?

- What do I do with the interesting information that I find?

- How do I use the things I find to help develop my own pedagogy?

Following

If you have been able to explore and search productively, you will have found key people and key sources of ideas that you will need to follow. Your personal learning network is beginning to grow. At this point you will need to be quite critical. It is easy for your network to grow too quickly and become too noisy (i.e. there is too much stuff there and it becomes difficult to see the wood for the trees). This is particularly true for you as a teacher. You do not have the luxury of time on your hands. It is also too easy to surround your network with comforting voices that underpin your own viewpoint. Although there is nothing intrinsically wrong with this, it will be important for you to follow people or sources of information that provide challenge to your own thinking (as grit within an oyster produces a pearl). So you will regularly need to ask some hard questions about the people and sources within your personal learning network.

REFLECTIVE QUESTIONS

- Is this person or source providing high-quality information that I am finding useful within my personal learning network?

- Are the key messages from any one person or source targeted specifically? Or is there too much 'noise' around their feed of information that makes it difficult for me to ascertain what is valuable?

- Is there an appropriate degree of challenge to my own way of thinking from my sources?

Tuning

Tuning your personal learning network is a vital behaviour and needs to be done regularly. Think about this in relationship to an analogue radio signal within a car radio. Whilst it might work perfectly in one area, as you travel across the country it gradually weakens and gets noisier until it is lost completely. It will need retuning, manually or automatically, to maintain its signal quality. The same is true within a personal learning network. You will need to evaluate your key sources over time. As the power of one specific source fades, you will need to either re-tune or delete that signal in favour of another. Having too many tired or weak signals will just weigh down your network and mean that key messages are hidden within too much background noise.

REFLECTIVE QUESTIONS

- Is the quality of input from your key people or sources being maintained over time?

- What adjustments do I need to make to my personal learning network in order to maintain its clarity and usefulness?

Feeding

Feeding is about building relationships with others within your personal learning network. Up to this point, we have put you at the centre of the network. Through the key behaviours of exploring, searching, following and tuning, we have argued that you can build a personal learning network that benefits you and your teaching. Feeding is about giving stuff out to your network, rather than just receiving stuff in. Here, basic aspects of human communication apply. As you make contact and share interesting stuff, people will respond and share good stuff with you. As you are open and generous with your time and resources, so you will find that others will be towards you. The key point here that Rheingold is at pains to emphasise is that you need to be proactive within your personal learning network. Share first. Do not wait for someone you are connected with to share something with you. Take the initiative. Give, and things will be given to you. Become known as someone who gives more than they receive within your network. This is the key to creating a rich personal learning network of your own.

REFLECTIVE QUESTIONS

■ What can I share within my personal learning network?

■ How can I be more generous with my own ideas and resources about teaching within my network?

Engaging

Engaging goes beyond feeding and giving. It is about using your personal learning network to go beyond basic sharing of ideas and information, to share insights and experiences at a deeper level with those who you trust. Rheingold's work here reminds us of the importance of being kind and courteous in our engagement with others. Many of our interactions are done through words (although increasingly images and video are coming into play). When we cannot see someone in cyberspace, little words like 'please' and 'thank you' are vitally important in communication, and will really mark you out as a teacher who wants to engage seriously with others. As importantly, they will help create a learning network that it is enjoyable to spend time within.

REFLECTIVE QUESTIONS

■ What are the hallmarks of a quality communication and engagement with someone online?

How can I build on the strengths of my own communication with others in the 'real' world and ensure high standards are maintained within my engagement with others online?

Enquiring

Feeding and engaging with the ideas of other teachers within your personal learning network are the first level of interaction. Enquiring and responding (see below) can be conceptualised as a second level of communication or interaction. Enquiring about others and their wellbeing builds value in our relationships. This is as true in our face-to-face relationships as it is online. Being mindful about others and their work will enrich your personal learning network and, as we saw in our discussion around feeding your network, will result in a richer form of communication and support for yourself as a result.

REFLECTIVE QUESTIONS

How can I build time into my working life to enquire about others and their work within my own personal learning network?

How do the basic human interactions that I have developed over time in my face-to-face relationships translate into a personal learning network where others are, in one sense, more remote and the standard forms of expression do not apply so easily?

Responding

Responding appropriately to others within your personal learning network is Rheingold's final suggestion for us to consider. As people engage with you and enquire about your work, be responsive and take the opportunity to build strong and meaningful connections with others. If someone takes the time to write a comment on your blog, acknowledge it and thank them and, more than that, engage with their points in a constructive way. Build capacity and strength in that particular node of your personal learning network. It will never be time wasted. But as important as the content of the message is the way it is transmitted. Ensure that you set a good example and influence your network with a positive tone at all times.

REFLECTIVE QUESTIONS

■ What kinds of response would I like to receive from the enquiries I make within my personal learning network? How can I model these in my own responses to others who contact me?

■ More broadly, how can I set a good example for others within my personal learning network?

Summary

This chapter examines how an understanding of connections in networks helps to explain the world we live in. It raises a number of questions about learning, formal and informal, in schools and outside them. Let's try to draw some of these questions together.

We have seen that networks are not hierarchies. At least, they do not need to be supported by hierarchies. Because of this, they encourage a kind of collective exploration, chaotic by nature but not stifled by a top-down, rigid, one-size-fits-all procedure. The internet, in particular, is associated with social autonomy – with freedom over the choices that are available, including the choice of what, where, when and how something is learnt. Networks also encourage a more social, relational 'culture of learning' to emerge (Thomas and Brown, 2011), where it is possible to connect, to access sources of information and join communities seamlessly across the network. Those communities need not be simulated or artificial, but can be authentic communities where problems are discussed and solutions offered by the network. Do learners harness the power of these communities and this culture of learning? Do they do so in school?

Christakis and Fowler (2010) have shown us that networks give rise to phenomena that are not present in individuals: that networks exhibit their own fluid intelligence. Castells (2004) emphasises that knowledge is generated by combining and recombining such intelligence. All around us we see mass connections between people and information in dynamic networks. They consume, construct and share knowledge. How similar is this to how the creation of knowledge is understood currently in schools and universities? Are we perhaps too concerned with the ways in which individuals accumulate knowledge, and too little with how knowledge is constructed through connection? How could sharing as learning can be embedded in our curricula and pedagogy?

Connectivism, a new theory of how learning takes place in a connected world, has provided us with a framework about how learning works in networks and how learning might be fostered in networks. There is an implicit suggestion of the democratic nature of learning which can fundamentally democratise education. Once connected, the

the network is neutral; poverty and social disadvantage are not themselves impediments to accessing high-quality educational experiences. Rather than the skills to connect, it is, following Castells, those skills that enable learners to understand and nurture the network, which will be vital in the future. These new network skills, often referred to as twenty-first-century skills, are those most likely to prepare people to learn in and through their connections. What, then, are those skills and how do we encourage learners to develop them?

In Chapter 4 we look at how connectivism can be translated into a pedagogy through looking at network practices (those online activities that most closely ally themselves with connectivism and networked learning), as well as more traditional approaches to your pedagogy, your school and its local context. All these form part of a network within which you, and your students, are an integral part. Understanding your position, as well as that of your students, within this network, and how the flow of information moves within it, is an essential part of becoming an effective educator in the twenty-first century.

Networks thrive when information circulates through them. Circulating information by sharing is the first of these network skills, to which we now turn.

Notes

1   www.sometics.com/en/sociogram
2   oracleofbacon.org
3   www.imdb.com
4   www.framinghamheartstudy.org

References

Backstrom, L. (2011). 'Anatomy of Facebook'. www.facebook.com/notes/facebook-data-team/anatomy-of-facebook/10150388519243859 [last accessed 1/8/14].

Barabási, A. L. S. (2002). *Linked: The new science of networks*. Cambridge, MA, Perseus.

Caldarelli, G. C. M. (2012). *Networks: A very short introduction*. Oxford, Oxford University Press.

Castells, M. (2004). *The Network Society: A cross-cultural perspective*. Cheltenham, UK, Edward Elgar.

Christakis, N. A. and Fowler, J. H. (2010). *Connected: The surprising power of our social networks and how they shape our lives*. London, HarperPress.

Dobbin, C. and London Transport Museum (2012). *London Underground Maps: Art, design and cartography*. Farnham, Lund Humphries.

Dodds, P. S., Muhammad, R. and Watts, D. J. (2003). 'An experimental study of search in global social networks'. *Science* 301 (5634), 827–829.

Downes, S. (2005). 'An introduction to connective knowledge'. *Stephen's Web*, 22 December. www.downes.ca/cgi-bin/page.cgi?post=33034 [last accessed 02/08/14].

Granovetter, M. S. (1974). *Getting a Job: A study of contacts and careers*. Cambridge, MA, Harvard University Press.

Granovetter, M. (1983). 'The strength of weak ties: a network theory revisited'. *Sociological Theory* 1, 201–233.

Krebs, V. (2002). 'Uncloaking terrorist networks'. *First Monday* 7 (4).

Lynskey, D. (2014). 'Going underground'. *The Guardian* 3 February. www.theguardian.com/culture/culturevultureblog/2006/feb/03/post51 [last accessed 4/11/14].

Marineau, R. (1989). *Jacob Levy Moreno, 1889–1974: Father of psychodrama, sociometry, and group psychotherapy*. London, Routledge.

Moreno, J. L. (1941). *Foundations of Sociometry: An introduction*. New York, Beacon House.

Rheingold, H. (2014). *Net Smart: How to thrive online*. Cambridge, MA, MIT Press.

Siemens, G. (2005). 'Connectivism: A learning theory for the digital age'. www.itdl.org/journal/jan_05/article01.htm [last accessed 1/2/15].

Sparrow, M. K. (1991). 'The application of network analysis to criminal intelligence: an assessment of the prospects'. *Social Networks* 13 (3), 251–274.

Thomas, D. and Brown, J. S. (2011). *A New Culture of Learning: Cultivating the imagination for a world of constant change*. Lexington, KY, CreateSpace.

Travers, J. and Milgram, S. (1969). 'An experimental study of the small world problem'. Sociometry 32 (4), 425–443.

Ugander, J., Karrer, B., Backstrom L. and Marlow, C. (2011). 'The anatomy of the Facebook social graph'. arxiv.org/abs/1111.4503

Uzzi, B. S. J. (2005). 'Collaboration and creativity: the small world problem'. *American Journal of Sociology* 111 (2), 447–504.

Wilson, C. (2010). 'Searching for Saddam.' *Slate* February. www.slate.com/articles/news_and_politics/searching_for_saddam/2010/02/searching_for_saddam_5.html [last accessed 2/6/2014].

3 Sharing and curating

KEY QUESTIONS

- Why do we share our knowledge?
- What is content curation?
- How can I develop a personal learning network of my own?

Introduction

Why do you share your knowledge? This probably seems like a strange question to reflect on as a teacher. Isn't teaching about sharing knowledge? And if not, what then are we supposed to be doing? Are we 'delivering the curriculum', 'meeting the learning objectives', or even, perhaps, 'managing behaviours'?

If you think you do share knowledge, what is it you share? Who do you share it with? How do you go about doing it? In your working world, who shares their knowledge with you? Who prefers to keep knowledge to themselves or to use it for themselves? Would you describe your working environment as being a sharing one?

Do you share your knowledge online? If not, is it because:

- You worry what others might think of your ideas?

- Without an 'audience' you feel that sharing online is sharing into the void?

- You lack confidence?

- You worry what other colleagues might think?

- You are afraid of being mediocre, wrong, or an imitation of what other, more 'famous' voices are saying?

- You feel vulnerable?

These are all questions, feelings and arguments that we have grappled with as we have shared our own work over the years. In this chapter, we look at the question of knowledge sharing through a wider lens in order to understand a little more about the nature of sharing, about why we share, who we share with, and how we could share more effectively.

Sharing as social exchange

During the 1980s I lived in Italy, teaching at the university, playing football in a local team, rock climbing with a local club and generally hanging out in the bars, piazza and trattoria. It was a convivial community. Its hub was a local bar, and its superconnectors were the owners, Luca and Roberta. So when anybody needed something, or something done (from borrowing a van to help with local government bureaucracy, a bit of plumbing or dentistry) either you knew someone who had what you needed or who could do what you needed done for you. If not, then Luca or Roberta would broker a meeting with someone over a glass of wine. There was no monetary payment involved. Instead, people shared their knowledge and expertise. My expertise was translation between English and Italian, and I rarely said no. This was a sharing economy in which not only each and every person paid back for favours received, they also paid forward for favours they anticipated asking for in the future. These were not 'services' that were exchanged, in the sense that the *Yellow Pages* are a source of services in an anonymous marketplace. It was the reciprocal exchange of things, knowledge and skills. I could translate, and so help someone solve a particular problem they had. I knew the UK, so could offer advice and guidance to anyone planning a trip or holiday.

Of course, there were those who received more than they offered, as well as those whose actual knowledge or skills failed to match the level claimed. These people were slowly, often imperceptibly, marginalised. They disappeared from the community and hung out in a different bar. Those who remained nurtured their reputations as the currency that enabled their inclusion and allowed the community to thrive. As we saw in Chapter 2, the individual thrives when the community thrives. The more embedded you are in a network, the more likely you are to contribute to that network. Vitally, when there was real need, nobody in the community withheld their knowledge or ability to help.

In Chapter 2 we also looked at how important network structure is in shaping individual behaviour and how, when the individual thrives, so does the network. The same situation can be seen above, but from a different perspective. The community that I describe from my experiences in Italy is one that facilitated the flow of information, support and social norms. These can all be thought of as social resources and 'assets'; in the literature of sociology they are referred to as 'social capital'. Because the group I hung out with in Italy was rich in these assets, sociologists refer to it has having a lot of social capital. Here's a more formal definition of social capital:

features of social organisations, such as trust, norms [or reciprocity], and networks [of civil engagement], that can improve the efficiency of society by facilitating co-ordinated actions. (Putnam et al, 1993)

It is a simple idea which helps to explain why human or financial capital might be neither necessary nor sufficient for encouraging collective action or community involvement. The key difference between social capital and other forms of capital is that social capital is embedded in the fabric of our groups and communities. Human capital and financial capital are based on individuals or assets, while social capital lies in the relationships between individuals and in the connections they have with their communities.

What Putnam reminds us with this concept (and what I learnt in Italy) is that we are more likely to share our knowledge, skills and experiences when embedded in a network that is rich in social capital. The secret to increasing social capital is trust and norms of reciprocity: if we don't agree how to share, how to give and take, or if we don't trust each other and have no mechanisms for measuring that trust, then we are all that much poorer.

Developing a sharing economy

The bar in Italy during the early 1980s was a small-scale cooperative community where goods and services were shared in ways that balanced personal self-interest with the wellbeing of the community. We knew, as did many communities, that sharing stuff created great communities. If the idea got a little lost over the past twenty years, it has emerged with perhaps greater strength and urgency more recently. The 'sharing economy' is being held up as the model for effective, sustainable production and consumption for the future. People are now sharing bicycles, cars, textbooks, houses, money, clothes, tools, dogs, nannies and even grannies on an unprecedented scale. Books such as *What's Mine is Yours* (Botsman 2010) and *The Mesh* (Gansky 2010); web-based companies exploring the latest shareables; and online magazines such as *Shareable*[1] suggest that the groundswell of support for sharing may have reached a tipping point.

In a sense, the movement is a natural extension of the kinds of experience I documented in Italy. The relationships that are built through sharing resources are as significant as the resources themselves: Airbnb (an online community marketplace for accommodation throughout the world) is not simply about the quality of the accommodation. It is built and sustained by the relationships between the people in the community who use it. Bicycle, car and clothes sharing may also be a response to an anti-waste ethic where buying, using and burning is being replaced by a greener recycling conscience which has political as well as cultural overtones. And, of course, sharing saves money. In the context of an economic recession, sharing a nanny will be more popular when childcare costs can run into hundreds of pounds a month.

If the cultural and economic conditions have been favourable to sharing, it has been the technical infrastructure of the web that has enabled them to flourish. This infrastructure was always envisioned as primarily a place to share by the inventor himself:

> The dream behind the Web is of a common information space in which we communicate by sharing information. (Berners-Lee 1998)

Mobile technologies with geo-location services linked to social networks have allowed people to coordinate their sharing with greater and greater precision. Online social networks are today's word-of-mouth, where strong and weak ties combine to extend the reach of local communities. Because trust is the oil that allows sharing in a community, mechanisms for enabling trust to thrive online are constantly in development. Escrow legal agreements; the integration of users' social graph (Facebook + LinkedIn + Google+) to establish identity; ratings systems; and reputation engines (such as TrustCloud) are all designed to establish 'reputation capital' (Botsman 2010) in order to build trust between strangers.

If we consider the global spread of platforms such as StreetBank, Kickstarter and Etsy, it seems to be working very well. Nor is its success such a great surprise if we consider the emergence of 'social production' and its spread through online networks. Open source software (where code has been written and shared in communities of software engineers) has been used to build the platforms that are driving this sharing economy. It was such software that led to the development of Napster in 1999, the platform that pioneered peer-to-peer file sharing. Its philosophy contributed to establishing Wikipedia as well as sites such as Flickr, YouTube and SlideShare. In turn, these mass-sharing hubs laid the foundations for the new generation of real-time sharing through platforms such as Twitter, Instagram and Foursquare.

Our students may be unfamiliar with the details of the history of commons-based resource sharing on the web. However, they have all inherited the technical infrastructure and cultural practices based on it: they more naturally 'access' than buy, 'share' rather than own. They stream music on Spotify or Pandora, access newspapers online, and subscribe to TV programmes and films through watch-again services and companies such as Netflix.

In short, our students are primed for sharing.

REFLECTIVE TASK

If our students are primed for sharing (and they are), have you ever thought of teaching as sharing? Why is it that you want to become, or have become, a teacher? What is it that you want to share with your students that led you to make this important decision? What would be the benefits of this sharing for your students and for yourself? How can a sharing community or economy be established in your school?

Why we share

Sharing extends well beyond our role as teachers. We will shortly come on to the specific inferences for this debate regarding the processes of teaching and learning when we examine personal learning networks in more detail. But, for now, the research in this area provides some valuable insights on why we share, which are worth dwelling on further. If the social, economic and technical foundations are present for sharing to emerge, what are the personal motivations to share?

Sharing as an act of kindness

When we share, we not only help someone, we also say something about ourselves and the person we share with. 'I found this interesting, I think you will too.' It's a gift. When we give a gift, we assume it has some value and relevance to the person we're giving it to. When it does, then our reputation in their eyes is enhanced. When our reputation is enhanced, we're more trusted and our relationship with that person is strengthened. When we get it wrong, when what we give has no value or relevance to the person, then our reputation suffers and our relationship with that person weakens. That can also happen when giving a gift is confused with exchange. Giving gifts does not entail favours in return. It can result in favours, but these by-products are not built in to the giving. If favours are expected, that can undermine the nature of the gift and the relationships that emerge from the giving.

Christakis and Fowler (whose 2010 book *Connected* we looked at in Chapter 2) discovered that this kind of sharing not only enhances reputations, it also triggers other acts of sharing. They set up an experimental study to examine the theory that social networks influence the spread of cooperation (Fowler and Christakis 2010). In that study they showed that when one person gives money to help someone else, the recipient of the cash becomes more likely to give away their own money. In the group situation they describe, this leads to a cascade of generosity in which the itch to cooperate spreads first to three people, then to the nine people with whom those three people interact, then to everyone else. This is an important pattern: when one person experiences the positive benefits of sharing for themselves and the group with which they interact, the motivation of others to share is increased.

Sharing as an act of kindness enhances reputation and, in a domino effect, can spread throughout a group of people. Of course, selfishness can also spread in a similar way. The question for our work as teachers is, which pattern do we want to provoke? Which culture do we want to participate in? A culture of gift-giving where our knowledge is openly shared with others, or one where knowledge is selfishly hoarded and the hiding of expertise is encouraged?

Sharing for recognition

When you began this chapter and were thinking about what knowledge you share and what you keep to yourself, you may have made a distinction similar to that made by the subjects of a study by Constant, Keisler and Sproull (Constant et al 1994). They found that employees distinguished between two types of knowledge that they shared at work. One type concerned 'products' such as reports that had been commissioned and that they had been required to write. The second type was experiential: knowledge that they had learnt from their experiences of working in the organisation. This type of knowledge they considered to be part of their professional identity.

When it came to sharing their knowledge, the researchers discovered that the motivations were different for each type. People shared reports because they were considered intellectual and physical property of the company. They shared their experience because they received personal recognition for doing so. This recognition came not in the form of a pay rise or promotion, but from peer recognition and respect. The fact that peer recognition is seen as more important than recognition by a boss is important here, and not as counter-intuitive as it might at first seem. The manager may be a gatekeeper to wealth and promotion, but she may not understand the value of your experience in the same way as other people who do the same work as you. When a peer says 'Ask Jenny about that, she really knows what she's talking about', then Jenny is likely to feel highly valued and respected.

Sharing as communion

I regularly share novels I've read. Not all of them, but certainly the ones that have really affected or changed me in some way. When I do, the offer is mostly expressed with the phrase: 'You *must* read this, it'll completely change the way you think of X.' It seems that I'm not alone in this. In an oft-quoted study on sharing, Jonah Berger and Katherine Milkman studied over 7,000 online articles from *The New York Times* to examine which were shared most by email and why (Berger and Milkman 2010). Not only did they discover that people shared more positive than negative stories, and more longer, intellectually demanding articles than shorter, simpler pieces, they also found that the stories most often shared were 'awe-inspiring'. By this they meant stories that were large-scale and changed the way the reader saw the world. They suggested that the reason why such stories are shared is the 'emotional communion' that results from it. This is the idea that when you read something that has a real emotional impact on yourself, which changes you and changes the way you see the world, then you want to share that feeling. When was the last time you shared for emotional communion?

Sharing to learn

One of the biggest difficulties we face with students coming into the first year of university is to challenge their idea that learning is somehow about gaining competitive advantage. Many seem to think that in order to succeed, someone else has to fail. It takes time to convince them that by sharing what they know, they can enhance their learning.

In the period between primary school and university, they may have been taught how they need to protect their knowledge from others, to hoard it, because, as we are constantly reminded by first-year undergraduates, 'knowledge is power'. It takes some time to prove to them the more nuanced view that knowledge *shared* is power.

One way of doing this is to show how the bookmarking site Delicious works. Initially, students are interested in the idea that by moving their bookmarks/favourites from their own computers into the Cloud they can access them from anywhere. Yet still some students say that little has changed and that they prefer to access these saved pages from their own machine. In a way they are right. They haven't added any value by accessing bookmarks from the Cloud rather than from their own computer. However, once we move on to showing them how those bookmarks are shared and interconnected, new value is created which transcends and also fuels the act of bookmarking.

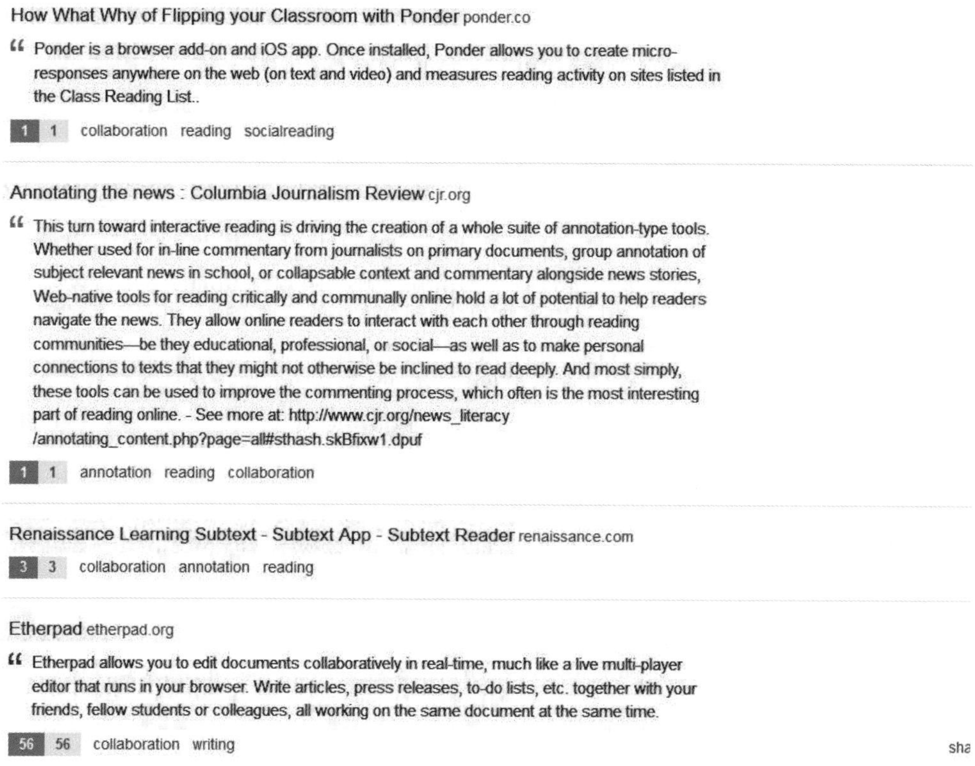

How What Why of Flipping your Classroom with Ponder ponder.co

❝ Ponder is a browser add-on and iOS app. Once installed, Ponder allows you to create micro-responses anywhere on the web (on text and video) and measures reading activity on sites listed in the Class Reading List..

`1` `1`   collaboration   reading   socialreading

Annotating the news : Columbia Journalism Review cjr.org

❝ This turn toward interactive reading is driving the creation of a whole suite of annotation-type tools. Whether used for in-line commentary from journalists on primary documents, group annotation of subject relevant news in school, or collapsable context and commentary alongside news stories, Web-native tools for reading critically and communally online hold a lot of potential to help readers navigate the news. They allow online readers to interact with each other through reading communities—be they educational, professional, or social—as well as to make personal connections to texts that they might not otherwise be inclined to read deeply. And most simply, these tools can be used to improve the commenting process, which often is the most interesting part of reading online. - See more at: http://www.cjr.org/news_literacy/annotating_content.php?page=all#sthash.skBfixw1.dpuf

`1` `1`   annotation   reading   collaboration

Renaissance Learning Subtext - Subtext App - Subtext Reader renaissance.com

`3` `3`   collaboration   annotation   reading

Etherpad etherpad.org

❝ Etherpad allows you to edit documents collaboratively in real-time, much like a live multi-player editor that runs in your browser. Write articles, press releases, to-do lists, etc. together with your friends, fellow students or colleagues, all working on the same document at the same time.

`56` `56`   collaboration   writing   sha

Figure 3.1 Screenshot of author's Delicious bookmark page

Students begin to use Delicious not just to find websites that they've forgotten the URLs of. They use Delicious to search for sites from within a network of trusted connections. They learn from sharing. Individual self-interest is perfectly balanced with the health of the community.

A visual and aural example of the same principle is provided by the project In Bb,[2] in which people were invited to upload a YouTube video lasting between one and two minutes in which they sing or play an instrument in B flat major. These small additions are then aggregated into a grid-like interface where the videos can be played simultaneously, and the soundtracks work together.

It's a simple and effective way of showing how sharing common acts both empowers the individuals doing the sharing and adds value to the group, which in this case becomes a kind of dynamic orchestra.

Platforms such as Delicious and YouTube are part of a wide raft of ever-increasing web resources that harness this power of sharing in order to add value to the group.

REFLECTIVE TASK

Do any of these motivations for sharing have a direct correlation to your work as a teacher? Whilst sharing to learn might be the most obvious correlation, to what extent could your students' or your own sense of self-esteem, self-regulation and confidence be boosted by sharing being conceived as an act of kindness, a source of recognition or an emotional communion?

Personal learning networks – a shared approach to teaching and learning

A personal learning network is the way in which you organise your learning through connections with social and informational networks. Putting it slightly more grandly, Couros writes that:

> Personal learning networks are the sum of all social capital and connections that result in the development and facilitation of a personal learning environment. (Couros 2010: 125)

Although a personal learning network might include tools that help you organise your work (such as using Evernote to store ideas, Scrivener to write lesson materials or Moodle to host educational materials), these technologies in and of themselves are not a personal learning network. Personal learning networks go beyond the organisational and help you develop new knowledge, information and skills through engagement with others and their ideas. In other words, a personal learning network is a social network as well as a purely informational or organisational network.

A personal learning network is more than a collection of tools. It is about your knowledge, skill and understanding of the web, and how these can be used constructively to help shape teaching and learning processes.

Auditing your competence in this area is an important first step towards developing new skills. After all, if you don't know where your strengths and weaknesses are, how can you constructively seek to improve yourself? Fortunately, many large companies such as Microsoft, Mozilla and Google provide frameworks to help you explore your own web competencies in various ways. As part of its work to support education, Mozilla has produced a set of competencies and skills that it (and its stakeholders) believe are important to pay attention to and get better at as you read, write and participate on the web.[3] These competencies and skills are listed under three main headings: exploring, building and connecting (given in full in Appendix 1). Use them as an audit of your own skills and competence in these areas. Which areas are you strong in? Which areas do you need to broaden your skills or competence within? Which are most important for teaching, in your opinion?

As we read through these statements, we had our own views about which related best to the teaching we do within our university. Clearly, some of the statements have specific applications within technical contexts that might not be relevant to your work. But the vast majority will touch on your work as a teacher in some way.

When you have completed the audit of your skills, you should be able to identify those areas that need strengthening or developing. This is where the resource is most powerful. For each of the key competence areas, Mozilla has produced a set of training materials to help you develop that skill further. Here we briefly consider 'Navigation' as one of the simpler competencies; after all, we can all use a web browser – right?

Like our competence with any tool, we can all learn to use a web browser more skilfully. For most of us, a web browser is the software that we use to interface with and explore the web. Given that we are all busy people with a lot to do every day, sharpening and developing our skills of navigation with a web browser will make us, and our teaching, more productive. Within the help section devoted to navigation[4] we are given an overview of what a web browser can help us do (under the heading 'Discover'); a summary of the key skills we will develop in order to use it better; and, most importantly, tips about how to shape and mould the tool (in this case, the web browser) to our specific requirements as a teacher (under the heading 'Make'). The final section of the help resource is 'Teach'. Here you and other teachers can access and submit helpful materials to help contextualise the knowledge, skills and understanding of this particular web competence for yourself and others.

Whilst Mozilla is not the only company that is producing this kind of educational guide to web competencies, we have found this set of resources to be particularly helpful and would highly recommend them to you as you begin to build your own skills and create your own personal learning network.

Auditing your web competencies using a framework of ideas and support materials like these are an important first step in building a personal learning network. When people think about building a personal learning network online, they tend to think first of tools. The problem is the plethora of desktop-based, portable, mobile and web-based tools that already exist, and the number of tools that are being introduced to that list on a weekly basis. It is very easy to drown in tool overload. Resources such as Mozilla's toolkit emphasise the importance of developing skills and appropriate understanding around key competencies rather than focussing primarily on the tools themselves.

To put it another way, building a personal learning network to help underpin and inform your teaching is not about adopting specific tools (although tools of the type we explore in the next part of this chapter will be important). It is more about a mindset or set of behaviours that you need to identify, adopt and apply to your work as a teacher.

However, tools are important. In Appendix 2 we provide a list of some of the basic tools available today that will help you construct your own personal learning network. Have a look at those before you undertake the following Practical Task.

PRACTICAL TASK

The task is to construct your own personal learning network using some of the above tools, and any others that you have noted when reading this book. Spend some time acquainting yourself with how your chosen tools operate, and personalising them to your own specific needs. Think about how the various tools you have chosen connect together, and try to integrate them within the technology you have available in a constructive way.

Alongside the tools that will underpin your personal learning network, there are various online tools that can help you map it, too. Using these tools constructively can become another important element that will allow you to tune your network in the way that Rheingold (2014) suggests. They enable you to make sense of the various interrelationships that you are constructing in your network. Some of the dedicated network analysis software is complicated and requires advanced programming capability. Some, however, can be very simple to use.

You could start with your Facebook friends. Netvizz[5] is a Facebook app that looks at all your Facebook friends and sees who is friends with whom. You can map your LinkedIn network with socilab.com and your Twitter network with mentionmapp.com.

Here are a few final pieces of advice about your personal learning network.

Firstly, work in the open. Teaching is too often characterised as a private activity, something that takes place behind the closed door of your classroom. Whilst writing this chapter, we heard about one teacher who was complaining about her headteacher, who used to make unannounced visits to her classroom. She found this threatening and difficult to cope with. Whilst we can quite imagine a set of circumstances where this could be problematic, for the vast majority of teachers we would suggest that having a physical open door to your classroom is always beneficial. Welcome any visitor to your classroom – senior school leader, fellow teaching colleague, parent or student – and share your own and your students' work. Adopt the same principle with your online profile. The more public you make your work, the more opportunities there will be for people to make connections with you, and the better and more productive your network will become.

Secondly, feedback on your network and the work that it helps you facilitate is vital. Develop a trusted, smaller group of friends who can give you honest input and feedback. We do this in our work, in terms of both our teaching in the university and our writing (such as this book). We actively encourage open, constructive and critical feedback on our work from this trusted group of friends. The benefits are immense.

Finally, resist the urge to conform in terms of your thinking. Actively move out of your comfort zone on occasions. Engage with different perspectives and find people to disagree with (politely). Proverbs 27:17 tells us that 'as iron sharpens iron, so one person sharpens another'. In constructing your personal learning network, you are committing yourself to a process of self-improvement and pedagogical development. You are demonstrating a whole range of professional attributes that mark you out as a teacher who is serious about their work and wants to develop further. You will find like-minded teachers out there who want to do the same. You can help each other, and spark off each other too. Enjoy the journey, and who knows where it will take you.

Why did that go viral?

Personal learning networks help us link our teaching with the wider world. At their heart, they are about sharing. We share because we like giving, because it enhances our reputation, enables us to cooperate with others, and so adds to our knowledge. But what kind of things do we share most of all? This has been a central question for marketing since the discipline emerged in the middle of the twentieth century. In his book *Contagious*, Jonah Berger brings together his own and others' research into why ideas, products and behaviours catch on and spread quickly. He wants to know why things go viral; what is it about some ideas that make them ripe for sharing or imitating? If we can explain social pandemics, the argument goes, we could go some way towards being able to create them (Berger 2013).

Understandably, the promise of revealing the secrets of how to make something go viral caused a great deal of buzz in marketing communities. Yet there may also be some suggestions in this research that can help us as educators. Knowing the factors that help explain social pandemics might be valuable for understanding how best to share those ideas that we, as teachers, want to spread. Berger suggests that there are six such factors: social currency, triggers, emotion, public, practical and stories. Let's look briefly at each trigger and consider their possible importance to our work as educators.

Social currency

We have examined this already in this chapter. Social currency refers to the reputation we gain in sharing with others. If sharing particular things makes us look more knowledgeable in the eyes of the group with whom we share those things, and knowledge is a value to the group, then we'll continue to share. Share a remarkable anecdote about yourself with your class that illustrates a point you are trying to make, and that anecdote is likely to be repeated and passed on. Its association with the point you were trying to make will go with it. That kind of anecdote can also create a sense of insider status for the group you tell it to. If you feel you are somehow special, that you have received something of value, then you are more likely to pass it on.

Triggers

We share what we are thinking about, and we think about what we can remember. When we associate an idea with something in the environment and then come across that something, we also remember the idea. A lot of learning is about establishing associations, creating the dots in such a way that they can be more easily connected together. One example of such a hook was established by my father struggling to remember to take his omega-3 supplements. He tried all kinds of ways until he connected the problem to his kitchen table placemat. He put the supplement on the top of the placemat and studied it carefully. After that, the placemat wasn't complete until the supplement was at the top right-hand corner. Creating these hooks, connecting the dots, is a lot like creating the habits that lead to the kinds of behaviour you are trying to establish.

Emotion

Anyone who has watched the television programme *Britain's Got Talent* will understand how arousing strong emotions (positive and negative) increases the possibility that something will go viral. One hundred and twenty million people viewed the video of Susan Boyle's first performance on *Britain's Got Talent* and it became YouTube's top video for 2009. Learning that has an emotional aspect, or that harnesses strong feelings, is likely to spread more than learning that evokes less arousing emotions.

Publicity

Phenomena that are in the public eye are more likely to be talked about and imitated than those that are more private. Celebrity culture is premised on this notion. In learning, we might want to challenge the current content of the public sphere in ways that could allow it to be populated by alternative ideas. We have seen this happening to charity giving over the past decade. Once a very private activity, it has now entered the public sphere and spread so that the activity of giving is mainstream, whether through the BBC's 'Red Nose Day' or websites such as Just Giving. Perhaps as educators we need to consider those values and behaviours that we want to move into the public sphere in order that they might become more spreadable.

Practicality

Ideas spread when they are helpful to other people. This is why 'How to' videos are shared so much. It is why 'The best of ...' lists get shared, and why educational videos such as those produced by the Khan Academy are passed on so enthusiastically. Just asking what is the practical value of an idea or product or behaviour will lead towards a consideration of how it might spread. Explaining the practical value of something is the first step in priming it to be shared.

Stories

We are a story-telling species and so packaging ideas into stories will increase the possibility that they are passed on. Products are now rarely advertised in order to increase sales. Instead, they are wrapped inside short stories, narratives that are memorable and will get people talking about them. One recent and very popular example of this is the Christmas advertisements for the John Lewis store.

What Berger and his colleagues have been at pains to explain is social influence; what makes certain ideas more popular than others. The six factors that we have explored above explain how this process works and helps us develop our understanding, enabling us to consider our own work as teachers and increase its social influence.

PRACTICAL TASK

Take one or two of the above triggers and think about a lesson that you are going to teach during the next week. For an example, we will take the 'emotion' and 'stories' triggers and combine them together.

Build the trigger(s) into the sequence of the lesson activities. In this example, this might require you to bring a story of some personal and emotional significance into the lesson. Use these as triggers to create a connection with your students in a way that perhaps you might not have been able to do if the story had been omitted. Don't force the issue though.

Over the coming weeks, see what, if any, impact the inclusion of that story has had on your students. Use gentle prompts to see if they remember the story. Has it been passed on to anyone else who wasn't in the class themselves? (As parents, we often hear about stories that teachers have told to our children when they are having tea or engaged in a family game of some sort.)

Ask yourself, what are the implications for your teaching over the longer term as you begin to incorporate a more deliberate strategy to develop ideas that are ripe for sharing by your students?

So far, we have seen the importance of sharing as gift-giving, as a new economic paradigm, as a way of achieving recognition and reputation, as a way of learning, and as a way of spreading ideas. Whilst we see the act of sharing as essential for education, we want to turn our attention now to the activity of sharing. To do that, we will introduce another perspective to inform our understanding: that of curation and the work of the curator.

Teaching as curation

There is a strong case for arguing that the word 'curation' has become something of a buzzword over the past five years and, as such, has almost become devoid of meaning. Its use has certainly increased rapidly. Google's Ngram Viewer shows this trend graphically in its yearly count of the use of 'curation' across a corpus of 5.2 million books digitised by Google up to 2008.

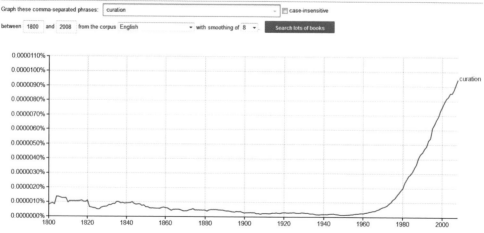

Figure 3.2 Google Ngram Viewer

It's not only in books where the currency of the word has increased. Now it seems that anyone who manages an event that brings together ideas, artefacts or even people is worthy of the title 'curator': people for parties and books for shelves are 'curated'. Even cooking is becoming an opportunity to curate a number of seemingly disparate ingredients. Online, we are continually petitioned to curate our profile pages on Google or Facebook, our photographs on Flickr, or even our preferences in living room make-overs on Pinterest. Marketing has championed this idea of curation, hyperbole for the rather nebulous expression of personal taste exhibited for the world to see.

However, there is another argument that we would like to make here. This is that the discipline of curation, as a metaphor and a set of values and practices, can be usefully used to think through the nature and importance of sharing in the field of education. The parallels and analogies come less from the world of ephemeral taste and marketing and more from the roots of the word and how it became associated with collections, exhibitions, museums and art galleries.

The word curation actually entered the English language in the late fourteenth century to mean 'one who has the cure of souls' (OED). In other words, a curator is a kind of spiritual guide. It was only in the seventeenth century that the word began to be used as an official title for the chief keeper in charge of a museum, library or art gallery, and with it was included the idea of preservation. Interestingly, the modern museum itself grows out of a tradition of curation that began with the Kunstkammern (or Wunderkammern) in Renaissance Europe. These were rooms (later cabinets) of curiosity, containing eclectic collections of natural, scientific, ethnographic and 'wonderful' objects that reflected their creators' interests and obsessions. Today's Ashmolean Museum is built on the collections of John Tradescant whose Musaeum Tradescantianum was the first museum to open to the public in England. Tradescant was our prototype curator. Throughout the seventeenth century he travelled in Europe, Russia, Turkey, Egypt and Algeria collecting seeds, bulbs (he was a gardener and garden designer to the rich and powerful) and curiosities, as well as managing collections bequeathed to him by friends.

The great difference between the early Kunstkammern and the museums and galleries they spawned lies in the categorisation and organisation of the collections they house. Whilst the former were juxtapositions of disparate objects expressing a singular idiosyncratic taste, the latter became organised collections of objects that have cultural, historic or scientific importance. It is in the modern museum and, relatively recently, the rise of the accredited curator that our idea of what curators do has been formed (Kuoni 2001).

So, the curator is the person who looks around the art world to find the finest works available and gathers those works together around a unified theme. The curator then embeds the theme inside a framework for the understanding of those artists' meanings and hosts a conversation around the resulting collection. The kinds of roles that such a description demands include: collector, classifier, meaning-maker, catalyst (for dialogue between the artist/object and the audience/

public), and intermediary (between such groups as artists, audiences, institutions, funders, collectors, dealers, buyers, press, publishers, photographers, other curators). We might also think of contemporary curators as 'editors'. In the same way as a book's editor would assemble, arrange and oversee an author's ideas (and in an edited collection the ideas of a number of authors), so curators also assemble art and cultural practices, sharing them with audiences through exhibitions as well as events, talks, educational programmes, catalogues and other publications (Smith 2012). How well they do this ensures or questions their reputation and credibility as institutions and professionals.

In the 1990s the 'independent curator' emerged from the museums and art galleries. Instead of working in accordance with the edicts of particular institutions, the freelance curator uses skills and knowledge that are independent of particular collections or stewardship of permanent works. For some, these skills and knowledge mean that the curator is more author of meaning than purveyor of the meanings of others. The distinction can be a source of conflict: whose meaning should be privileged in an exhibition space? The artists, the providers of the space, or the curator? The tension is between somehow facilitating the meanings of others and responding autonomously in a presentation of those meanings to others.

If the curator is an author, should curating also be considered a creative activity? This issue has led to the rise of the auteur-curator and curator-artist (O'Neill 2012). In the world of film criticism, the word *auteur* refers to the central role of the director as the creator of the film. It is the director's vision or 'world view' that the film ultimately communicates, unified through the collective efforts of those actors, writers, and back-room staff who are named as the credits roll. This is the viewpoint that has achieved cultural prominence: it is Steven Spielberg, Tim Burton or Quentin Tarantino who is celebrated for his creativity and authorial vision. Applied to curation, it might imply that the curator uses the artist or subsumes the work of art to their particular vision. However, less negatively and more usefully, the term invites us to see the whole process of creating meaning as one of combination, of a bringing together, of assembly where creativity sits neither on one nor the other side of the binary curator-artist, but actually on the hyphen.

In charting the rise of the curator, even in this very brief vignette, we are beginning to see some roles that resonate with the world of education: the curator as guide, as discerning collector and sharer of diverse sources; as frame-maker for understanding; as maker and creative author of new meaning. However, in the words of Nick Waterloo we find the most suggestive expression of those values in curatorial thinking that extend far beyond the confines of galleries and museums, and link the curator with educational activity more generally. Chillingly prescient, they were found by his wife in a notebook next to their bed shortly after his death in 2009.

A Curator's last will and testament

1 Passion;
2 An eye of discernment;
3 An empty vessel;
4 An ability to be uncertain;
5 Belief in the necessity of art and artists;
6 A medium – bringing a passionate and informed understanding of works of art to an audience in ways that will stimulate, inspire, question;
7 Making possible the altering of perception.

(Kuoni 2001)

As two educationalists interested in sharing knowledge in the context of education, we might explore these values in the following way.

Passion

Passion is starry-eyed. It's obstinate and intense and can move enthusiasm into obsession. Its synonym is not 'engagement'. Sir Ken Robinson recognises the role of passion in education in his book *The Element: How Finding Your Passion Changes Everything* (Robinson 2009). The central premise of the book is that currently neither students nor teachers are finding their passions in schools. They are not discovering fulfilment through following their talents, ambitions and interests. Educational policies are not allowing teachers to build those spaces where 'natural aptitude can meet personal passion', which is how Robinson defines 'the element'. Change is needed.

An eye of discernment

Discernment concerns critical judgement. It's not a word that is used often in the educational literature, but the idea it references is a core competence. Critical inquiry is premised on discernment. Media literacy requires it. Effective teaching is built on it. Being able to judge whether or not an activity worked, or whether or not the introduction of a particular piece of knowledge was appropriate, depends on discernment.

An empty vessel

Prejudice and preconception can be obstacles to the discovery and learning of new ideas, of meeting new people and exploring new landscapes. As teachers, being truly receptive entails being empty in that sense. This is a difficult position to adopt as a teacher. It could be perceived as weakness. But, in truth, it is a position of great strength that can lead to powerful and meaningful encounters with others (students) that will transform their lives as well as your own.

An ability to be uncertain

Certainty closes debate. It can lead at best to conviction and authoritativeness, and at worst arrogance and absolutism. An ability to be uncertain stimulates curiosity and inquiry, the roots of learning.

Belief in the necessity of art and artists /
A medium – bringing a passionate and informed understanding of works of art to an audience in ways that will stimulate, inspire, question

These values may seem very specific. However, if we simply substitute learning for art; teaching for artists; and students for audience, we produce something that speaks to a particular vision for education: Belief in the necessity of learning and teaching. A medium – bringing a passionate and informed understanding of learning to students in ways that will stimulate, inspire, question.

Making possible the altering of perception

We've all had the aha! moment of seeing either the old lady or young woman in the famous optical illusion (Figure 3.3).

Figure 3.3 Optical illusion: what do you see, young woman or old lady?

But when you are able to create the conditions for that moment to occur is when you are able to change the way somebody sees the world. It is a very powerful moment and lies, we would argue, at the heart of teaching.

These are some of the values and practices that curation, as it emerged from museums and art galleries, shares with education. However, trends have emerged in the past ten years that have made the analogy even more useful:

- We have started to drown in a flood of online information;

- In order to find stuff online, we have begun to integrate our social networks with search engine algorithms;

- Social media platforms have provided users with the tools to curate and share content.

As a result, we have seen a rise in online content curation: the extension of the curator analogy into the messy world of the web. As schools have begun to build web resources into their teaching programmes, the consequences of the above three points have often pushed many schools and teachers to breaking point.

In 2013 Intel calculated that in one minute of time on the internet:

- 204 million emails are sent;

- Facebook is viewed six million times and logged into 277,000 times;

- Google receives more than two million search queries;

- 1.3 million videos are viewed on YouTube;

- 47,000 apps are downloaded;

- 3,000 photographs are uploaded to Flickr;

- 100,000 new Tweets are sent.

And that's in *one* minute. The number of networked devices today is equivalent to the total global population. By the time you are reading this the figure will have doubled (as will most likely the number of messages on social media sites that are produced by robots).

It is this constant stream of content, the individual textual, audio, image and video data distributed through platforms such as blogs, video and image repositories and citizen journalism sites, together with collaboratively produced content on such sites as Wikipedia, which leads to claims that we are being deafened by the noise of our own activity. We can't take it in, and unless we are able to find, collect, organise and make it useful, vast amounts of information, ideas and conversations which are 'out there' will remain 'out there'. The web is a messy place and the difficulty of finding stuff there is a very real one.

The problem has existed since the birth of the web as a collection of horizontally organised and inter-linked documents. Software engineers initially tackled it by trying to categorise websites into discrete directories. This was the preferred solution of Yahoo in the early days, when people thought the web could actually be classified in this way. With the explosion in the number of sites and the difficulty of determining the relative importance of one site with respect to another, Yahoo's directory structure was doomed to failure. People very quickly began to look more for particular bits of information contained on pages on the web, rather than for websites. Google came up with a system for collecting together pages on the web that responded to this problem and completely by-passed the need for human-created directories and categories. Instead, they used an algorithm to rank individual pages based on the links to and from those pages. Google indexes the pages on the web and allows users to search the index, returning results as a list of ranked pages. Its mission has echoes of the curator and the Kunstkammern: 'to organise the world's information and make it universally accessible and useful'.[6]

That same algorithm enabled Google to popularise aggregation (bringing together content produced elsewhere into a single page) through Google News and Google Reader. Google News provides thousands of news stories from online sources organised to reflect interest in news from the UK, Europe, the world, business, sport etc. With Google Reader (closed by Google in July 2013), users could create their own news pages by subscribing to feeds from various news sources, all filtered according to Google's search algorithm. This use of feeds (RSS) meant that content from different pages could be easily brought together and presented according to various machine-determined criteria. Algorithmic strategies were beginning to look as if they could make sense and meaning out of the vast swathes of hyper-connected documents.

However, if Google revolutionised the way in which we find information, its PageRank algorithm has struggled with a different problem that people on the web began to have with the emergence of a more personal, social web in the last five years. The problem of finding stuff changed to the problem of finding people, or people to connect to, or conversations to participate in as online social networking blossomed. This challenge was most obviously met by Facebook. Its curation of the web was based on its newsfeed: status updates from friends, including links to what they were doing on and offline. Now people were finding information from their friends as much, if not more, than from Google. Finding people to connect to becomes more important than information itself. Facebook recognises this with its suggestions as to friends you might connect with. As we saw when examining networks, connecting to the 'right' people means you have the possibility of connecting to the 'right' information. Facebook's social graph then becomes the new algorithm for finding information. The importance of the solution was not lost on Google, which launched Google+ in 2011. The slight difference in emphasis was that Google+ concentrated not on organising the web by sharing with a mass group of friends, but on targeted sharing with various social groups organised into 'Circles'. However, the Holy Grail for these companies remains the same: providing a one-stop platform for finding and sharing content on the web.

The biggest problem with both Facebook's and Google's algorithm is that the social graph it produces is symmetrical: you can 'friend' a person only if they agree to have you as their friend. The inbuilt bias of Facebook is that you connect with close friends, or that all your connections are close friends. There is nothing nuanced about 'friends' on Facebook. Once the connection is made, you see each other's content. On Twitter, that is not the case. Twitter offers another method of finding information through people by allowing asymmetrical connections: following someone on Twitter does not imply being followed by them. You choose what information you want to receive without the obligation to follow anyone. Many people find information on the web through their Twitter network. This is true not only for breaking news and trends, but also for specific content and conversations through hashtags and Twitter lists. In fact, Twitter describes itself as an information network, not a social network. Whilst the information flows are different, both Facebook and Twitter are platforms that have integrated social networks with algorithms in order to filter relevant and interesting content for their users.

The latest trend that has contributed to the rise of online content curation has been the ways in which social media platforms have encouraged users to curate content by providing them with the tools to do so.

Media theorist Steven Johnson saw this phenomenon emerging over ten years ago with the introduction of the iTunes celebrity playlist feature. He argued that in 2003 Apple had unwittingly opened the possibility of a 'curatorial culture' where people with great taste in music could share their selections (Johnson 2003). Since then, social media platforms have curated content by giving curation tools to users. YouTube introduced playlists to enable people to bundle their favourite videos together; Flickr offered galleries; and Amazon introduced Listmania lists, suggesting that they were tapping into the frenzy for curation. These platforms either employ their own algorithms to curate things such as Channels auto-generated by YouTube, or business news via LinkedIn Today, or they encourage users to tag content or use hashtags and lists on Twitter.

More recently, dedicated platforms have emerged together with leading content curators, drawing our attention to and contextualising the interesting and useful. Some of these have made an impressive impact. Pinterest now has seventy million users worldwide (Horwitz 2013); Storify is now used by media groups such as the BBC, Al-Jazeera and *The New York Times*; and Scoop.it has attracted considerable interest from digital marketing consultants. Self-describing content curators such as Jason Kottke,[7] Maria Popova[8] and Longform[9] are increasingly seen as 'agenda setters' through their judicious selecting, framing and sharing of content through extensive online networks.

In essence, these latest tools and the people using them effectively are merging the best of algorithmic filtering with human, social ordering and making sense. They are providing a solution to what Clay Shirky famously referred to as 'filter failure' (Juskalian 2014), which we have all experienced when we feel overwhelmed by the plethora of available information vying for our attention. Shirky argues that the idea of information overload (the result of opening up publishing on the web to everyone with a connection to the internet) is in fact a misnomer. Instead, what the feeling refers to is an inability to navigate information flows in ways we associated with library catalogues or high-street bookshops. During the past ten years, we have been experimenting with new paradigms to replace the library catalogues and linear, alphabetical encyclopedias. The current iteration, these content curation platforms for information discovery, dissemination and discussion, allows everyone to filter the river of hyperlinked multimedia into small eddies into which we can swim and tread water for a while, knowing that the contents of the pool are worthwhile spending some time exploring. We are beginning to harness our online networks actively to generate ideas and produce knowledge.

In the next section we look at some practical suggestions as to how you might get started creating and nurturing your networks, and curating content for those networks and your students. Specifically, we consider how to use some of the tools that we introduced earlier in this chapter as part of your personal learning network.

A curation workflow

Collecting content and sources

The first thing anyone interested in curating information does is to collect online content together with the sources of that content. The distinction between content and sources is an important one. I may come across a blog post that I think is relevant and insightful about a topic I am interested in. I may come across another from the same blog, and then another. I soon realise that blog is itself an important source of content that I need to monitor. Content and sources in blogs, from news sites, video platforms, Twitter personalities or Twitter lists, all need to be collected together and monitored. Curators set up systems so that information comes to them when it is updated rather than having to go to each individual website to check on updates. These systems rely on social and cognitive skills: being able to ask the right questions, with the right vocabulary, and embedded in a collaborative network of people, are vital prerequisites for effective curation. We will deal with these aspects in depth when we look at the digital literacy implicit in the connected classroom in Chapter 4. Here, let's continue looking at the technical or media-specific literacy needed to establish these systems.

Two technical components make it easier to manage information online: RSS and persistent searches. RSS (Real Simple Syndication) allows searching to become collecting: it turns around the concept of looking for something so that the 'something' is actually looking for you. Facebook newsfeeds use RSS to deliver the updates of all your Facebook friends into your newsfeed. It's a feed, a channel or river of information, the content of which is determined by which RSS feeds you subscribe to, that is, which friends you include in your flow. Blocking friends, silencing them or unfriending them are all ways of curating your friendship group (your network) on Facebook so that you receive information that is relevant and valuable to your wants and needs.

RSS is powerful and can revolutionise the ways in which you discover information online. When an RSS feed is available, normally linked through this icon,

you can subscribe to future updates. Those updates can be brought together, aggregated, on a variety of 'feed readers'. There are hundreds of different ones and there will be many more variations on the theme in the years to come. We look at some of these in Chapter 4, but simply to illustrate the use of feed readers, Figure 3.4 shows Feedly, a reader we currently use to collect together a variety of information from various sources.

Figure 3.4 Feedly

Persistent searching and alerts

The second technical component to finding content and sources is persistent searching or alerts. The web is an information network that is changing every second, as we saw at the beginning of this section. Searching the network for information this morning may give a completely different set of results from searching it this afternoon. To cover this eventuality, we need a search query that is always looking for results and enables us to decide when those results are most conveniently received. Google provides this service, which can be easily integrated into your feed reader.[10]

Twitter hashtags (which are themselves curated channels aggregating Tweets from different users), users and lists each have RSS feeds that can also be incorporated as persistent searches. More about Twitter when we look at teaching in a connected classroom (Chapter 4) and look in detail at mapping people and conversations. Now that we have established systems for discovering new content and sources for content, we can sit back and watch the river flow. We have created a stream or channel through which relevant information comes to us. It will need tweaking in order to get the filters right. We will also have to learn not to think we have to read everything that comes our way. It's a river, and we need to get comfortable with the idea of both wading in up to our chest and dipping our toes in tentatively; we rarely always read everything. But we do need to read.

Personalising content

As we read, we begin to make sense of the information and evaluate it. The next step is to select those items that are most relevant to our 'audience'. It may be for ourselves, for a class, or for a group of colleagues with whom we are involved in professional development. Knowing the audience means we can personalise the content, adding context and meaning. Changing the title of an article may bring our readers' attention to it more quickly; using an image may focus readers on a particular aspect that we are interested in emphasising. Juxtaposing one item with another will itself shape the way that both are perceived. Our criteria for making the selection may be as wide as 'interestingness' (Maria Popova) or as narrow as 'Updating reading list for the BA (Hons) unit, communication and social care'. We select by using our passion for and critical understandings of the area, together with a deep appreciation of the needs of our audiences.

Sharing our content

Next, our selections are shared with our audience. Over the years we have used a variety of platforms to share content with students – from email distribution lists to blogs, learning management systems (such as Blackboard and Moodle), social bookmarking (Delicious and Diigo), Facebook pages and dashboards (Netvibes, iGoogle). However, one tool has emerged recently that easily and intuitively enables many of the characteristics of the best kind of online curation, and that illustrates individual and collective content sharing. Scoop.it is a good place to start experimenting with this kind of collection and sharing of information. Figure 3.5 shows a screenshot of a recent Scoop.it page that I have been using with students on a communication unit looking at network activism.

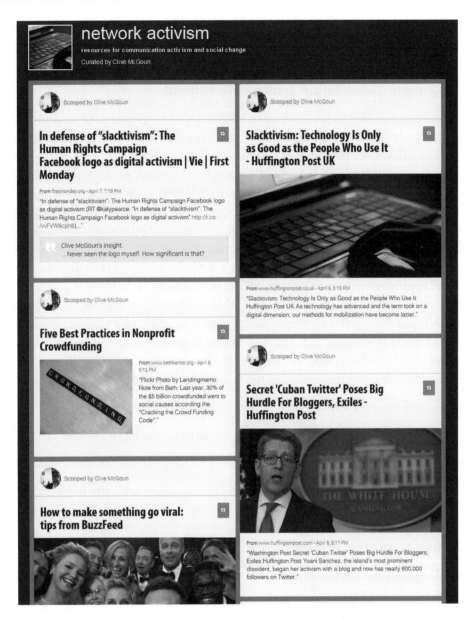

Figure 3.5 Screenshot of author's Scoop.it

Not only is this page or board shared directly with students, it is also embedded in my own blog, the students' learning management system, and unit Facebook pages. Notifications of when new items are added are distributed automatically through Twitter and emails. Newsletter-style emails can easily be generated to share content on a weekly basis. However, more than simply making sharing easy, Scoop.it incorporates other essential features of the curation work flow. Stories are not 'scooped' in their entirety. You get the link and can put your own interpretation and emphasis on it. So it is very easy to change the image accompanying the post or add one if none was originally used, add a 'teaser' to attract your readership, frame a particular story for your readers, and explain what you expect them to learn from it.

Developing a conversation around the content

In our discussion of curation, we have been keen to emphasise the importance of hosting conversations about the collection. Through its comment streams for each post, Scoop.it allows the curator to nurture discussion around particular topics. The quality of discussion generated is one of the clues as to how readers are interacting with the content of the collection. In addition, Scoop.it allows usage of the page you create to be tracked, enabling the curator to generate some fine-grained feedback that can be used to fine tune the collection to better meet the needs of its users. Finally, it is also possible to work with a community of co-curators in Scoop. it, either on a single collection or through a network of curators exploring similar topics. Tapping into the work of other content curators with similar passions is a great way to develop your own. Those other content curators may be experts in their fields, or they may be your students exploring topics for the first time. What we are all doing is learning and sharing together in ways that harness our networked, distributed information and transform it into knowledge.

So, a curation workflow includes the following elements:

- Collecting: sources and content;
- Filtering: creating an information eddy relevant to needs;
- Selecting: deciding what to share;
- Framing: creating ways of understanding and working with the item;
- Sharing;
- Hosting: creating a discussion space;
- Tracking: understanding engagement with the collection, to enable fine-tuning.

PRACTICAL TASK

Identify a topic that you are going to teach in a forthcoming lesson, perhaps a few weeks in advance. Draw together the main content, and sources for that content, and work through the various stages identified above. Although we have talked about curation here in the context of online curation, it could be that you want to translate these ideas into a physical environment, such as the construction of a new display within your classroom where content can be aggregated and presented, and through which a discussion can be facilitated. You might also want to think about an online site for your newly formed curated content, such as a Wiki page on your school website.

Summary

This chapter began by interrogating the extent to which we share our knowledge and whether as teachers we might share it more effectively. We have used a wide-angle lens to examine some fundamental shifts in sharing practices brought on, in part, by a technical infrastructure, the internet, which allows the easy formation of groups and networks. We applied some of these key thoughts to the establishment and operation of a personal learning network, and how specific tools can be used to help foster particular types of behaviour that will be beneficial for your teaching. Our exploration of the world of museum curation allowed us to establish some principles around the collection, display and sharing of artefacts which, we argue, is thought-provoking for the world of education generally. Those principles become even more pertinent as more and more of our knowledge artefacts are digital and stored on the web. The problem is transformed from being a 'keeper' of scarcity to being a manager of abundance. There are more resources that are relevant and valuable to our educational development than we could possibly read in ten lifetimes, let alone one. So far, the gateway to these resources has been dominated by Google's algorithm, despite efforts within education to encourage students to use library databases and institutional search engines. Slowly, online curation is beginning to augment the algorithm and re-introduce 'the human' as a gateway to digital resources. Whilst Google is not threatened by online curators, if enough people curate content online in the ways we have explored here, then perhaps Google's position as sole arbiter of visible knowledge online will be increasingly questioned.

Before we leave this chapter, we need to remember that online content curation is content re-use, the sharing of content produced by others. There are many different ways of doing this, from simply taking that content and re-publishing it elsewhere without any credit being given, to carefully transforming and/or re-purposing a source that is given full credit. One is plagiarism; the other is knowledge building. One is theft from one; the other is theft from many. With so many possibilities now for 'easy' sharing (driven more by the competition for attention and the needs of advertisers), we have to be very attentive to how we curate. We need to become curators whose reputation is effectively enhanced through the quality of our sharing and contribution to the discussions we host. We do that by constantly developing our digital literacies, practices such as critically engaging with media, managing, understanding and evaluating information, and participating in digital learning networks.

At the beginning of this chapter, we asked you whether or not you share your knowledge, and what blocks to sharing you might have met. Nobody, we would suggest, is immune to such blocks. No-one shares their knowledge without a certain amount of fear creeping in. As authors of this book, we are no different. What have been our fears and what are our ways of thinking through them?

People will laugh at what we think

This is always a possibility. It rarely bothered us when we were under five years old. It's bothering us less the older we get. However, the people we respect won't laugh.

Someone has said all this before

Well, as we argued, everything has been said before. Nothing is really original. So why are we worried?

We have nothing to say

This is the panic button, the insecurity that arises when we try to do something we haven't done before. It is irrelevant. We all have something to say. Refer back to the section on 'Making possible the altering of perception', which discusses how much information is uploaded to the web every minute.

What we have to say is not perfect

This fear is completely unrealistic. If all we shared were things that were perfect, we would be in big trouble. Good is not perfect. Inevitably, our work will be flawed: we are humans, after all.

We have not solved the problem of the fear of sharing our work, but we have understood a little more about where that fear originates and what strategies we can use to challenge it. And we keep David Bayles and Ted Orland's idea uppermost in our minds:

When you act out of fear, your fears come true. (Bayles and Orland 1993: 23)

Notes

1 www.shareable.net
2 www.inbflat.net
3 wiki.mozilla.org/Learning/WebLiteracyStandard/Legacy
4 webmaker.org/en-US/resources/literacy/weblit-Navigation
5 apps.facebook.com/netvizz
6 www.google.com/about/company
7 kottke.org
8 www.brainpickings.org
9 longform.org
10 google.co.uk/alerts

References

Bayles, D. and Orland, T. (1993). *Art & Fear: Observations on the perils (and rewards) of artmaking.* Santa Barbara, CA, Capra.

Berger, J. (2013). *Contagious.* London, Simon & Schuster.

Berger, J. and Milkman, K. L. (2010). *Social Transmission, Emotion, and the Virality of Online Content,* MSI Reports: Working Paper series 114. Cambridge, MA, Marketing Science Institute.

Berners-Lee, T. (1998). 'The World Wide Web: A very short personal history'. www.w3.org/People/Berners-Lee/ShortHistory.html [last accessed 9/5/14].

Botsman, R. R. R. (2010). *What's Mine is Yours: The rise of collaborative consumption.* New York, Harper Business.

Christakis, N. A. and Fowler, J. H. (2010). *Connected: The surprising power of our social networks and how they shape our lives.* London, HarperPress.

Constant, D., Kiesler, S. and Sproull, L. (1994). 'What's mine is ours, or is it? A study of attitudes about information sharing'. *Information Systems Research* 5 (4), 400–421.

Couros, A. (2010). 'Developing personal learning networks for open and social learning', in Veletsianos, G. (ed.), *Emerging Technologies in Distance Education.* Edmonton, AU Press, 109–128. www.aupress.ca/books/120177/ebook/06_Veletsianos_2010-Emerging_Technologies_in_Distance_Education.pdf [last accessed 2/10/13].

Fowler, J. H. and Christakis, N. A. (2010). 'Cooperative behavior cascades in human social networks'. *Proceedings of the National Academy of Sciences, USA* 107 (12), 5334–5338.

Gansky, L. (2010). *The Mesh: Why the future of business is sharing.* New York, Portfolio Penguin.

Horwitz, J. (2013). 'Semiocast: Pinterest now has 70 million users and is steadily gaining momentum outside the US'. *The Next Web* (TNW). thenextweb.com/socialmedia/2013/07/10/semiocast-pinterest-now-has-70-million-users-and-is-steadily-gaining-momentum-outside-the-us/ [last accessed 24/6/14].

Johnson, S. (2003). 'Judging 2003's ideas: the most overrated and underrated'. *The New York Times,* December 27. www.nytimes.com/2003/12/27/arts/27INTR.html [last accessed 4/6/14].

Juskalian, R. (2014). 'Interview with Clay Shirky, Part I'. *Columbia Journalism Review* December 19. www.cjr.org/overload/interview_with_clay_shirky_par.php [last accessed 14/6/14].

Kuoni, C. (2001). *Words of Wisdom: A curator's vade mecum on contemporary art.* New York, Independent Curators International.

OED Online (2014). 'curator, n.' *The Oxford English Dictionary.* Oxford University Press.

O'Neill, P. (2012). *The Culture of Curating and the Curating of Culture(s).* Cambridge MA, MIT Press.

Putnam, R. D., Leonardi, R. and Nanetti, R. (1993). *Making Democracy Work: Civic traditions in modern Italy.* Princeton, NJ, Princeton University Press.

Rheingold, H. (2014). *Net Smart: How to thrive online.* Cambridge, MA: MIT Press.

Robinson, K. A. L. (2009). *The Element: How finding your passion changes everything.* New York, Viking.

Smith, T. (2012). *Thinking Contemporary Curating.* New York, Independent Curators International.

4 Teaching and learning in a networked age

KEY QUESTIONS

- How can I use my personal learning network to help inform my classroom pedagogy?
- How does adopting a partnership approach facilitate teaching and learning in my work?

Introduction

CASE STUDY: THE EVOLUTION OF READING LISTS

Not so many years ago, our management of resources for the university courses we teach on consisted of updating a bibliography in September with new books that had been published during the year. It was a form of curation. We chose the books that went on this list according to established criteria that we had decided to adopt. They were organised, sometimes chronologically, sometimes alphabetically, but more often in terms of a reading route that we had planned through a particular part of the course. They were also shared. Photocopies were distributed, pinned onto noticeboards and occasionally even posted to students. This type of unit reading list still exists, but with a few important additions:

- Its content is largely digital. There are more digitised items on the list than paper books or journals;

- It's distributed exclusively digitally. We seldom see a student with a paper copy of the list. More often than not, we see it accessed on phones or tablets;

- It's dynamic; it will change, and not just at given points during the year.

This simple change in the format, structure and use of a bibliographical resource represents a significant change in how we, as lecturers, are presenting key information to our students. The consequences of the decisions we have taken to organise a reading list in this way are far-reaching and relate closely to many of the themes of this book.

However, they are not an end point. There are many further ways in which our reading list and its construction, sharing and use can be developed.

What would happen if we asked students to choose the reading list? What if we allowed them to rate and review each item on the reading list? What if the reading list was sortable by rating or review, rather than by what we, as lecturers, perceive as the 'correct' learning pathway within the unit. Would that be beneficial? Would we, as academics, and would our university, as our employer, be happy for these changes to be promoted? Do they represent a helpful or unhelpful step for the role of the university in the transaction or brokering of knowledge within our course?

In the previous chapters we have covered a lot of ground. We have explored key issues related to creativity, networking, sharing, curating and much more besides. We have shared insights from the literature related to each of these issues, and given examples from near and far to illustrate their implications for our thinking and practice. Along the way, we have provided a range of Reflective and Practical Tasks to help you apply some of these key issues to your own work as a teacher. In Chapter 3 we also explored how you could create your own personal learning network and use various tools to help develop, share and connect your teaching with others.

In this chapter we consider your pedagogy. We explore how your 'connectedness' through digital media and the web can help your work. Again, we take a practical approach and examples are given from the work of other teachers to help illustrate our key ideas. We also consider the teaching partnerships that you might want to develop in response to these key issues. As we have considered in detail in Chapter 2, the theory and thinking being networks and their power can be usefully applied to the world of education. We argue that this starts with you and your teaching, before moving outwards to the way you engage with and embrace opportunities for collaborative thinking and working within education.

The pedagogical context: teaching and learning within a networked classroom

The more we talk with children and teachers, the more music becomes entangled in lives and the more its significance fades in the light of experience. The closer we look at music events in schools **the more we see that music is the pretext – life is the text**. (Kushner 1999: 216; our emphasis)

Teachers lead by example. Substitute your subject area for the word 'music' in the above quote. In a very real sense, teachers do not teach their subjects. They teach themselves. Our demeanour, our attitude, our approach to others and the tools we use to educate ourselves are all laid bare in a classroom. Teaching is a wonderful privilege and one of the most important vocations that anyone can commit their life to. Why? We are shaping the lives of our children. We are not just teaching Music, Geography, Mathematics or whatever your subject happens to be. We are teaching them about life. For all these reasons and more, until we, as teachers, build our own personal learning networks and use them to participate in our own learning and connect with others, then we will not be able to help our students to develop these same digital skills to allow them to leverage the possibilities that online learning affords.

In the first half of this chapter, we consider some of the key themes of early chapters and relate these to your pedagogical approach in the classroom. As we have seen throughout our book, within the networked age, knowledge is published, distributed and shared in new ways. There are three kinds of content that can be published on a web page: content that has been created by someone; content that is pulled in to the page from a page somewhere else; and content that has been curated. Corrine Weisgerber (2014) uses an interesting analogy to elucidate the differences:

- Creation is like planting a seed from scratch;

- Aggregation gathers those seeds together;

- Curation sorts those seeds out, giving them a context so that they make sense.

We would add a further layer to the process of sharing those seeds through different channels. This is a process that has been outlined by Beth Kanter (2014), who herself built on a model of networked learning developed by Harold Jarche (2010). Kanter described a model built around three S's: seek, sense and share.

Seeking

There are many reasons why we might look for information. It might be for a particular topic within a GCSE specification, to follow up on a suggestion made by a student in a previous class, or to stimulate a particular group who you have found difficult to engage. Establishing these reasons is important. The more specific we can be about exactly what we are looking for and for whom, the more likely it is that we will find relevant and useful materials. Seeking will involve you in establishing effective search techniques that may begin with basic Google searches but then move, perhaps, into persistent open searches that harness RSS feeds or use your own personal learning networks. The information you can curate is only as good as the information you can find. Seeking and collecting knowledge, wherever you find it, is one of the key roles you undertake as a teacher. However, it does not end there.

Sensing

Making sense of the information that flows towards you from the queries you set up begins with aggregation. Aggregation is the most common form of curation, and involves bringing the most relevant information together into one place. There are two ways that this can be achieved online: through machine or human filters. Machine filters pull in information from automated searches and re-publish it on one website or blog. The process is automated through RSS feeds and, because it updates in real time, offers a real advantage over manually gathering information. A typical example of a feed aggregator is Google News. News from around the world is fed onto a single page hosted by Google. Generally such feed aggregators display the headline of a story and sometimes the first few lines of its content together with a link to the rest of the story on the website where it was originally published. Spigot[1] is an example of such an aggregator for research around learning, technology and youth. Aggregators of this kind generally use algorithms that sweep the web and bundle the latest news together. However, a lot of manual aggregation occurs on the web through blog posts that are simply lists of links (e.g. the 'Twenty-five best apps for education'), lists of reading material for courses, 'likes' and web pages tagged with various keywords.

Aggregation is not curation. Simply re-publishing or collecting information from different sources into one place is the first step in making sense of that information. The next step involves further filtering and contextualising the results of initial information queries. This contextualising can happen in a number of ways. Providing an introduction to the information may give a reason why it has been included and what its specific value is. The content might be distilled through summarising its main points. Connections might be made between it and other information. It might be arranged in a number of different ways: ranked, categorised, placed in a historical chronology, juxtaposed, or highlighted in a particular layout. As Robert Scoble said: 'A curator is an information chemist. He or she mixes atoms together to build an info-molecule and then adds value to that molecule' (Scoble 2010).

This mixing and adding value to information is your vital role as a teacher. Providing a list of URLs for your students to 'research' is not an effective teaching strategy. Students will need to be taught to make sense of what they can find online, how to rate the trustworthiness of particular sources, to make comparisons between them, to judge their timeliness or appropriateness, and much more besides. The aggregation metaphor can help you begin this process. However, there is much more than solely aggregation in your teaching and curating role.

Sharing

The whole point of curation is to feed a network. This network might be your personal learning network, or a network of students within your school that you are accessing via a virtual learning environment, or a class that is physically sitting in front of you. As we have seen throughout our book, sharing begins with spreading the news through our network. This might be a Tweet, a blog post, an explanation or a YouTube video. Following that, a space also needs to be created where conversations can be hosted, encouraged and animated. We need ways of stimulating participation and monitoring it in ways that we can use subsequently to improve the overall process.

Within our physical classrooms, we know how to do this skilfully. We can ask questions, provoke discussion, reflect on key points and use a range of general pedagogical strategies to facilitate the learning process. The same techniques are applicable online. As we share, and engage in online conversations about that sharing, we lay the foundations of a community of learning, but this will require our nurture and support if it is to have a sustained impact on our students.

Much of the conversation in the previous chapter was about you and the establishment of your own personal learning network. Clearly, at the point where you engage in the act of teaching about something and begin using some of these networked tools in the process, you are going to engage with students and their personal learning networks. Most students nowadays will have their own personal learning network. Generally, though, they do not call them that and they might not be as wise as we think they are in developing and nurturing them.

The personal learning networks that you can help your students create will be designed so that they can access the knowledge and learning materials that will help them to learn better. The whole point here is that the network will feed them stuff that they might not otherwise have discovered. This is central to your role as a teacher. What you and your students will quickly realise is that there is more value in social searching on networks than there is in utilising simple Google searches. As your own, and your students', personal learning networks grow and develop, you will notice a move away from algorithmic searches and the acknowledgement that the best knowledge and information comes from an understanding that people they are networked with share good stuff with them. In the following Reflective Task, we consider how this might work in the context of digital music, and how that is shared.

REFLECTIVE TASK

How do you or your students discover new music that you enjoy listening to? Think about the music services Spotify and iTunes. These have revolutionised how people find out about new music. You can listen to a 'radio channel' in Spotify. The music it plays is generated algorithmically according to the various tracks that you have listened to previously or perhaps have downloaded at some point. So far so good; connections are being made. You can also listen to playlists that someone else (human) has shared. Either way, the chances of finding new music that you enjoy are higher through curated content of one sort or another than by random selection. Translate this metaphor to other areas of knowledge acquisition. Finding out about things you don't know about now is done best when they emerge through networked processes rather than simple searches.

Before we move into the second half of this chapter and the focus on partnerships, it is important for us to dwell a little further on two highly personal aspects of teaching: teaching style and teaching role. Each of these is vitally connected to the opportunities for networked teaching and learning of the type we are promoting throughout this book. We will do this through two taxonomies, in one practical and one Reflective Task.

PRACTICAL TASK

Here is Mosston and Ashworth's (2002) taxonomy of teaching styles (Table 4.1). We are confident that these various styles will be easily understood by anyone who has spent more than a few hours in a school.

Table 4.1 Teaching styles

Teaching style	Meaning
Command	Teacher-centred exposition, 'chalk and talk', a type we have all experienced but which needs to be done in small doses.
Practice	The teacher sets tasks for students to practise throughout the episode.
Reciprocal	Students work in pairs, with one student giving feedback to the other. This can be applied to group work, too.
Self-check	The teacher establishes success criteria and the students work at their own level against these.
Inclusion	The teacher sets a range of tasks and students choose which they want to work on. (Please note that their use of this term is slightly different from current usage.)
Guided discovery	The teacher guides the learner towards a predetermined outcome, using questions and tasks within the learning episode.
Convergent discovery	One outcome is required, with the teacher guiding, if needed, their students towards this one outcome.
Divergent discovery	There are many outcomes possible, and the teacher supports, if needed, their students towards the discovering of one outcome (that may be very different from another student's in the class).
Learner designed	The teacher decides the topic area; the student chooses their own programme of study within it.
Learner initiated	The student decides what they wish to learn and organises how they will do it with the support of the teacher if needed.
Self-teach	Entirely independent with no teacher participation.

For each teaching style, try and identify at least one networked teaching and learning approach or tool that could be usefully brought alongside it to help develop it further within your teaching.

For example, how could a connected writing tool be used within the 'reciprocal teaching style' to help students work together in a meaningful way on a particular piece of writing? Alternatively, within a 'guided discovery' teaching approach, how could elements of a personal learning network be tagged in order to ensure each student is guided towards the desired end goal, but with a sense of emerging understanding along the way?

Following your work on the above, think about a lesson that you are going to teach in the near future. Choose one of the teaching styles and one of the networked teaching and learning approaches and tools, and write them into the heart of your plan for that lesson. Teach the lesson and evaluate the result. Then share the outcome with others within your personal learning network.

Stephen Downes, whose influence on the development of connectivism and connective knowledge was noted in Chapter 2, has recently outlined the multiple roles that teachers could play out within their classes. These are presented in Table 4.2 together with a brief explanation summarised from his work (Downes 2010).

Table 4.2 Teaching roles

Teaching role	Explanation
The learner	As someone who models the act of learning, the teacher helps students with this most fundamental of skills. This includes getting excited about something new, exploring it, trying it out and experimenting, engaging with it, and engaging with others learning about it.
The collector	Teachers have always been collectors, from the days when they would bring stacks of old magazines into class to the modern era as they share links, resources, new faces and new names. They find materials related to their own interests, keep in tune with student interests. They are the maven, the librarian, the journalist or the archivist.
The curator	One who organises and makes sense of that which has been found. The curator is like a caretaker and a preserver, but also a creator of meaning, guardian of knowledge, or an expert at knowing. A curator is a connoisseur, one who brings quality to the fore, one who sequences and presents.

Table 4.2 continued

Teaching role	Explanation
The alchemist	Mixes the ordinary and mundane into something new and unexpected. The alchemist practises the 'mix' of remix, the 'mash' of mash-up, the 'collage' of bricolage. The alchemist sees patterns and symmetries in distinct materials and brings them together to bring that out.
The programmer	Builds sequences into machines, manipulates symbols to produce meaning, calculates, orders, assembles and manages.
The salesperson	Plays an important role in providing information, supporting belief and motivating action. The salesperson is the champion of a cause or an idea.
The convener	The person who brings people together. A convener is a network builder, a community organiser. Conveners are leaders, coaches, and administrators; they are collaboration builders, coalition builders, enablers or sometimes even just pied pipers.
The coordinator	Organises the people or things that have been brought together for the common good. A coordinator is an eminently practical person, organising schedules, setting expectations, managing logistics, following up and solving problems. A connector and an integrator, but most of all a systems person.
The designer	Creates spaces for learning, whether in person, on paper or online. Designers attend to flow, perspectives, light, tone and shading.
The coach	Does everything from creating synergy and chemistry in a group to providing the game plan for learning, raising the bar and encouraging players to higher performance. Though the coach is on the side of the learner, in the learner's corner urging them on and giving advice, they also serve a larger or higher objective, working to achieve team or organisational goals.
The agitator	The person who creates the itch a person's education will eventually scratch. The role of the agitator is to create the seed of doubt, the sense of wonder, the feeling of urgency, the cry of outrage. Sometimes the devil's advocate, sometimes the revolutionary, sometimes the disruptive agent, and sometimes just somebody who is thinking outside the box.
The facilitator	Makes the learning space comfortable. Their role is to move the process or the conversation forward, but within a broad range of parameters that will stress clarity, order, inclusiveness and good judgement. The facilitator keeps things on track and, within reason, gently nudges things forward, but without typically imposing their own opinions or agenda onto the outcome.

Table 4.2 continued

Teaching role	Explanation
The moderator	Governs and prunes. The moderator of a forum is concerned about decorum, good behaviour and rules. They will tell people to 'shush' while the movie is playing, trim the trolls from the discussion thread, and gently suggest that the experienced pro ought to go more easily on the novice.
The critic	The person who asks for evidence, verifies the facts, assesses the reasoning and offers opinions. They are an aide to understanding, one who will extract the threads of a tangled presentation and make them clear. As logic texts everywhere proclaim, criticism consists first of exposition and only then of examination.
The lecturer	Has the responsibility for organising larger bodies of work or thought into a comprehensible whole, employing the skills of rhetoric and exposition to make the complex clear for the listener or reader.
The demonstrator	Demonstration has always been a part of education, whether a carpenter demonstrating proper mitring to an apprentice or a chemist demonstrating proper lab technique to a class. Traditionally, demonstration has been done in person, but today people who demonstrate can use actual equipment, simulations or video to tell their story.
The mentor	The role is multi-faceted, ranging from sharp critic to enthusiastic coach, but outweighing these is the personal dimension, the presence of the entire personality rather than some domain or discipline. Not everyone can be a mentor, not every mentor can take on too many prodigies, and of all the roles described here, that of the mentor is most likely to be honorary or voluntary.
The connector	Draws associations and makes inferences. The connector is the person who links distinct communities with one another, allowing ideas to flow from art to engineering, from database design to flower arranging. The connector sees things in common between disparate entities and draws that line between them, creating links and collaborations between otherwise isolated communities and disciplines. The connector sees emergent phenomena, patterns across different groups or different societies, or conversely identifies the unusual, unique or unexpected.

Table 4.2 continued

Teaching role	Explanation
The theoriser	Tries to describe how or why something is the case. The theoriser often works through abstraction and generalisation, which leads to critics saying they are not very practical, but without the theoriser we would have no recourse to very useful unseen phenomena such as mass, gravity or information. The theoriser is also the person who leads us to develop world views, finds the underlying cause or meaning of things, or creates order out of what appears to be chaos.
The sharer	Shares material from one person to another on a systematic basis. The sharer might be the person making e-portfolios available, managing the class mailing list, or passing along links and reflections from outside. But ultimately what the sharer offers most are cultures, concepts and ideas.
The evaluator	More than a marker of tests and assigner of grades – the evaluator assesses not merely declarative knowledge or compositional ability, but instinct and reactions, sociability, habits and attitudes.
The bureaucrat	Provides the statistics so necessary to the coordinator, manages the finances and resources, tracks the services needed by facilitators, organises accountability procedures and maintains systemic coherence.

REFLECTIVE QUESTIONS

■ What kind of teacher are you? Which of Downes' roles do you think best describes your own work?

■ Which one describes the work of other teachers who have taught you, or you've perhaps seen teaching recently?

■ How do you think the specific roles Downes identifies could help you create a networked approach within your teaching?

■ What are the consequences of the teaching roles outlined above for our students and how they learn?

Probably most of us will recognise a number of these roles within our own personality and role as a teacher. However, like any taxonomy, it challenges us to think about our comfort zone and imagine things differently. What would it be like to be the 'teacher as agitator'? How could I develop my teaching so I bring more of the 'teacher as alchemist' to the fore? Questions such as these will help you think differently about your role in the classroom, and this will have a bearing on how to begin to plan particular teaching episodes and re-imagine your role within them.

The partnership context: developing a new classroom through connections

In a general sense, making connections is a central ingredient of any form of partnership working. As we saw through our analysis of George Siemens' work in Chapter 2, connectivism builds on other learning theories, such as behaviourism, cognitivism and constructivism, by exploring the notion that much of your students' (and your own) learning takes place outside your head. It takes place in networks and through social connections. Learning is promoted as we embark on a process of connecting to, engaging with and participating in learning networks. Many of these will be online. But many will also be physical networks (as we saw earlier in this chapter when we considered how people portray their personal learning networks diagrammatically). Siemens' (2005) work teaches us that learning in this way is a cyclical process. The most powerful networked learning takes place when we connect to a network to find out new information, our understanding is developed through that engagement, and the fruits of that process are then shared back into that network.

However, there is one very important facet of connectivism that is highly relevant to our discussion here about partnerships. Connectivism is not solely about technology. It is principally about creating the conditions, space and opportunity for knowledge to be created. For this reason, we will now leave our discussions about how social media can be used to help form partnerships through connectivism, and turn our attention to a much more common form of partnership working in education.

Traditional approaches to partnership working

> Partnership working between schools has been a dominant feature of educational policy discourse for many years now both in the UK and internationally. (Higham and Yeomans 2009: 1)

Working in partnership is a key component of most schools' work today. These partnerships could involve other schools, local authority services, creative practitioners and local industry. But more importantly, these partnerships will also mean rethinking how we work with parents, carers, pupils and others. Schools should not see themselves, or be seen, as autonomous to the community in which they 'serve'. There are many forms of partnership that we can see in schools today.

A partnership of educational organisations

In the United Kingdom, partnership working encompasses diverse models, including initiatives such as the Leading Edge Partnership programme, the Specialist Schools and Academies model of schools working together around specialisms, and the development of cross-phase school partnerships to deliver wider programmes of work. Schools and universities work in partnership to deliver courses of initial teacher education as well as to provide access to higher-level academic qualifications.

A partnership for professional development

Many of the organisations listed above may have formed part of your own process of professional development. Your journey towards teaching has also been characterised by various partnerships. You will have combined academic study with personal beliefs and professional training. This training will have taken in knowledge and skills from key partners such as universities, schools where you have undertaken teaching placements, and perhaps other organisations too, such as subject associations or teaching unions. As you enter into school and work as a teacher, you become a partner in that school and bring to it your own personal skills and beliefs.

A partnership with students

It is the same too for the pupils who we teach. As Thomson (2002) argues, all students come to school with 'virtual schoolbags' of experiences, knowledge and resources developed in their lives outside school. Whilst this is easy to acknowledge, only some schools and teachers take the additional step and begin to draw upon their students' schoolbags in the construction of their curricula. This key point is important for us to consider as we set out our thoughts on partnership within a networked approach to teaching and learning. We need to consider carefully what parts of our 'schoolbags' are drawn upon, and whether this agrees with the principles we set out for what is important in our curriculum. Working in partnership should help us promote a more diverse sharing of ideas and a wider understanding of what is important in any given local community or learning network.

A partnership with parents

Parents and carers are vital in this mix. They are key educators of the students we teach. In this most obvious of partnerships, we need to work hard to make sure we work collaboratively. True partners do not work in opposing ways. Critically, the evidence from existing research and projects does not imply that parents should be tasked with taking on the role of formal educators; instead, the aim of such partnerships should be to work with parents to understand how they might bring their own distinctive expertise and resources to bear in the school setting. Clearly, there are obvious ways in which social media can begin to help bridge this potential divide. The challenge is not simply to harness parents to the existing goals of the school, but to enable educators to understand and engage with the resources that exist outside the school, and to engage with parents in a debate about curriculum design and purposes.

This could be seen as a key shift in how we approach all partners who may have bearing upon our curriculum in school. It is important to acknowledge at the beginning of this third and final section of this chapter that all partnerships, whoever they are with, need to be judged against how they bring their own distinctive expertise and resources to bear in the school setting. At the heart of this relationship there needs to be a shared understanding of what each partner can bring to this new curriculum. There needs to be a meaningful dialogue between the partners that results in a shared and understood vision of what being in 'partnership' means.

An area-based approach to partnership

Traditional approaches to partnership working in education such as those outlined above are fairly obvious and well understood. More recently, and primarily through the work of the RSA,[2] schools have begun to think about how they can use the resources of their locality to broaden educational opportunities. The RSA defines this 'area-based curriculum' approach as:

> An enhancement of the educational experiences of young people by creating rich connections with the communities, cities and cultures that surround them and by distributing the education effort across the people, organisations and institutions of a local area. (RSA 2009)

This definition has two main components. Firstly, it is about schools and teachers making connections with their local communities, villages, towns or cities and the various elements of their locality; secondly, it is about seeing education as something done in partnership with other people, organisations and institutions throughout their local area. In other words, it is about sharing responsibility for the education of our young people with a greater number of partners. Sharing the responsibility to educate our young people with others does not mean that schools should neglect their own responsibilities. Partnership working is good, but schools have a set of experiences, competencies and skills that other partners may not have; schools have to be able to quality assure the process and practice of an area-based curriculum offering when other partners are involved.

As the RSA has developed its work in this field, various alternative definitions and statements of what constitutes an area-based curriculum have evolved. Recent work describes an area-based curriculum as one that is:

- *About* a place: making use of local context and resources to frame learning;

- *By* a place: designed by schools in partnership with other local stakeholders;

- *For* a place: meeting the specific needs of children and local communities.

(RSA 2012: 5)

The RSA goes on to provide a set of objectives for an area-based curriculum, namely that it should:

- Create learning experiences that are engaging for children from all backgrounds;

- Increase children's understanding of and attachment to the place where they live;

- Embed schools more deeply within their communities and localities.

(ibid)

Here is our response to the above Reflective Task.

Educational partners

These might be organisations in your area that are there primarily to support your work in school. In the past, these may have included area coordinators for subjects or curriculum support teams based within local authorities. More recently, these will be organisations that have been recently privatised or are partially centrally funded, but also charged with a responsibility for supporting your school curriculum or national or local strategies. Included in this would be organisations such as music hubs or teaching schools within an alliance.

Business partners

Local businesses can become powerful partners for many reasons. A local business may already sponsor your school, or perhaps individual subjects in school have their own links to businesses in related areas. However, the benefits of business partners are wide-ranging. Try and think beyond the obvious links and be creative about the potential partnerships that local businesses might offer.

Voluntary sector partners

In your local area there will be a vast number of voluntary organisations that have a small amount of full-time staff supplemented by volunteers. They may include local heritage centres, transport museums, communities of artists, reading groups and other literary associations, organisations that work in early years or end-of-life care, and many more. These are the sorts of organisation that are used to working in partnership. It is how they grow and survive. They are also the types of organisation that schools have traditionally used for visits and other work.

National organisations

Although not always local to your school, many national organisations are supportive of the work done by schools and can help put you in touch with potential partners. These larger partners often find it difficult to find schools that are willing to work in partnership. They may offer 'calls' for partnership working via their websites or through particular projects that they want to develop. Keeping in touch with larger organisations like this is worthwhile via their websites and, if possible, through making contact with their education officer. Informal conversations and sharing information about your work with these organisations can often lead to exciting formal partnerships further down the road.

There are numerous case studies of this kind of area-based partnership in schools today. However, we include here an older example from Jonathan's work as a teacher at Debenham High School in Suffolk. Reflecting Others was a partnership-based project with a local arts agency and a young offenders' institution housed within an adult prison. The following case study explores what happened as students and young offenders learnt about each other without ever meeting face-to-face.

CASE STUDY: REFLECTING OTHERS – A DIGITAL COLLABORATION BETWEEN YOUNG PEOPLE IN TWO CONTRASTING ENVIRONMENTS

There are many more ways of expressing yourself rather than just talking. (Year 9 girl)

A central challenge for the education system is to find ways of embedding learning in a range of meaningful contexts where pupils can use their knowledge and skills creatively to make an impact on the world around them. (Seltzer and Bentley 1999: 10)

Music lessons for pupils in years 9 and 10 at Debenham High School were far from conventional during the autumn 2000 and spring 2001 terms. In them, you would have been as likely to find pupils working with digital video cameras, iMac computers, digital recorders and microphones as with traditional musical instruments. You would have found pupils recording the hustle and bustle of school life, the countryside, their hobbies and interests, collecting audio samples from CDs and radio programmes as well as visual images from the local skateboard park and leisure centre.

In another part of Suffolk, within a highly secure special unit, young offenders were offered the opportunity to carry out a similar exercise. Both pupils and young offenders documented, through sonic and visual digital recordings, their environment, sense of identity and community as young, twenty-first-century teenagers. After the collected materials were exchanged, they became source materials for a number of sonic and visual compositions made by one group about the other. They selected, edited and manipulated the images and sounds using a variety of innovative software tools. The sonic and visual compositions produced were arranged to make a specially designed sound and visual installation that was housed in the Exhibition Room at Snape Maltings Concert Hall. The installation was transferred to the school and the prison before returning to Snape Maltings for public viewing during that season's Aldeburgh Festival and Snape Proms.

This work, Reflecting Others, was an innovative digital arts project that had, at its heart, the idea of representing oneself and others through sound and image (a full analysis of the project can be found in Savage and Challis 2002). The project linked pupils in years 9 and 10 (aged between 13 and 15 years) with a small group of young offenders (aged between 15 and 18 years) in the Carlford Unit at HMP Hollesley Bay. Whilst the project involved the whole of year 9 (approximately eighty-four pupils with a full range of musical ability) and took place entirely within designated music curriculum time, the prison's group of young offenders was much smaller (approximately twelve) and was made up of volunteers. The school pupils did have some prior experience of digital technologies within their music lessons in the Dunwich Revisited project; the young offenders had little or no experience of this prior to the project, and worked within a designated two-hour session on a Friday afternoon. The project was organised by Aldeburgh Productions' Education Department and funded by The Monument Trust, with additional support from the J. Paul Getty Jr. Charitable Trust.

Reflecting Others used sonic and visual material collected from the pupils' and young offenders' actual environments. Three starting points (identity, community and environment) defined the process by which they selected material. The use of digital technologies was essential as a tool for gathering the material related to these responses. Pupils were able to use a MiniDisc player and digital video camera to collect material from any environment they chose, and subsequently to use it as source material for their pieces.

The material collected by the young offenders has fascinated pupils. This was evidenced by their rapt attention to the video artists' presentation of the video material (without sound) in the first lesson after Christmas. Pupils were very keen to ask questions about the daily routine in the life of a young offender, the offences they had committed (which they were not allowed to know about), and more general questions about the judicial system. The year 10 group were equally interested in the sonic material. Seemingly insignificant things, like the variety of young offenders' accents, were picked out by pupils as being of significant interest. The material content of some of the words and phrases used by the prisoners were commented on. Undoubtedly, some of the words and phrases the prisoners had recorded were there for shock effect. To counterbalance this, pupils received the recording of a prisoner reading, with obvious difficulty, a poem that he had written with quiet and sombre appreciation.

The young offenders viewed the pupils as 'little rich kids'. They found their accents interesting too; they commented on how plummy they sounded in comparison with theirs. The Carlford Unit is entirely male and there is no association with female prisoners. There could have been problems with female images within the male environment of the prison, and there were several comments made. The words and thoughts that the prisoners heard in the audio samples tempered these initial reactions. These turned the raw images into characters of pupils as real individuals. As the project continued we noticed a positive change in some of the prisoners' reactions to these visual materials. However, at no point during the project were pupils and young offenders able to meet, talk or contact one another.

One initial surprise was the similarity of responses between the two groups in certain areas. The two groups of project participants were of similar ages, had ranges of similar interests, and had a natural curiosity for images of the other sex. Examples of sonic and visual themes explored by both groups include:

■ Sports hall games, including basketball, badminton and squash;

■ Sounds of the cafeteria or lunch hall;

■ Weight and fitness rooms;

■ Recorded CD extracts of popular dance music.

But there were stark differences in the environment. The young offenders inhabited an internal space, with hardly any view of the outside world; the pupils were able to collect a much broader range of environmental material.

As teachers, we often asked ourselves the following question: how truthful are we being in calling our project Reflecting Others? Were we really encouraging pupils and young offenders to give considered reflection to the 'other' within their work? It was pleasing to note in discussion with pupils that they often felt a real affinity with the young offenders through the material they had collected. The following comment was fairly typical:

> I like it when they talked about the prison. That person described the place but it looked completely different. The 'Prisoner on the Moon' poem helped us to know what they feel like inside. (Year 10 girl)

Despite not being allowed any personal contact with the young offenders in any way, pupils did think deeply about the life of a young offender:

> By the looks of things it looks worse that I thought 'cos I expected they would be able to go outside and do more normal activities like we do. But they're trapped in there never seeing proper sunlight, trapped between walls, bars, gates and doors, trapped in Hollesley Bay for so many years and never going outside. They're looking at the same things day in, day out for years. I think this is wrong. And one boy's poem about the prison backed this up. No crime deserves to do this to a child. (Year 9 boy)

Comments like this impressed on us the value of choosing an appropriate starting point for any creative project. Providing a vehicle for pupils to challenge social agendas, for example, enables them to grasp a key ingredient of artistic expression – personal communication. So often musical composition within the classroom context is divorced from pupils' life experiences as teenagers and the real value that music plays for them in expressing their identity, sense of community and environment. But authentic artistic expression is inextricably tied to life itself:

> The more we talk with children and teachers the more music becomes entangled in lives and the more its significance fades in the light of experience. The closer we look at music events in schools the more we see that music is the pretext – life is the text. (Kushner 1999: 216)

As project leaders and teachers, we are only too aware of the pressures that we face in fulfilling the demands of a National Curriculum. But these comments show that pupils value a chance to use a variety of artistic expressions as a way of commenting and reflecting on their lives and others'.

The opportunity for pupils to work with a greater degree of autonomy, empowered with the tools for effective reflection on their artistic practice, was certainly an important element in the Reflecting Others project. Equally important was the collaborative activity within the project that was facilitated by community groups, including the local prison and Aldeburgh Productions.[3] This kind of partnership approach to the arts has a long tradition of providing 'educationally rich' experiences (Swanwick and Lawson 1999: 59).

In terms of the broader themes of this book, it is interesting that the Reflecting Others project demonstrates many of the strengths of a networked approach to teaching and learning well before the internet became common in schools. Students within the project were able to use basic digital technologies such as a MiniDisc player to collect sounds; these needed to be downloaded into a computer and curated so that another group of people could listen to them and make new music out of them; this sharing of digital content was reciprocated and the results were shared in a public space (the installation). The Reflecting Others project utilised many of the processes and ways of thinking that we have been considering throughout our book: connecting and collaborating with others, being creative, collecting, combining and re-mixing ideas, sharing, curating and hosting the products of our learning, learning together.

Interestingly, Jonathan was asked to visit the University of Cambridge to act as an external examiner for a PhD whilst we were putting the finishing touches to this book (in late 2014). After the viva, another lecturer from the Faculty of Education came up to him and said something along the lines of 'You won't remember me, but I remember visiting that installation you put together at the Snape Maltings Concert Hall.' Given that the installation was produced around thirteen years ago, this came as something of a shock. It served to remind us how powerful such approaches are within education and how they leave a mark on those who engage with them. However, this longer-term tracking of the impact of education on our lives is something that educational research has always struggled to deal with.

This account of the Reflecting Others project acts as a bridge for us in this chapter. It highlights and returns us back to the themes associated with technology and its use within a networked approach to education. In the project itself, there was a ceremonial exchange of computer hard disks between the school and the prison. This necessitated someone getting into a car and driving the twenty or so miles from Debenham to Hollesley. Today, digital content can be shared instantaneously. However, as our next case study shows, the processes of working with digital technologies need to be fully understood if we are to embrace them to the full in our partnership working.

Developing connections through subjects

Technology and social media can create connections between subjects in at least three ways: technologically, artistically and educationally. Firstly, technologically: as we have seen throughout our book there is an inherent potential for digital technologies to encourage connective ways of thinking and acting. Secondly, in the wider artistic world newer forms of technology have begun to transform what we might call traditional subject cultures in powerful ways. The Reflecting Others project discussed above is a good example of this. Additionally, what might be summarised as an 'inter-disciplinary' approach to the arts is obvious within subject cultures (Savage and Fautley 2010). These reflect ways of working within the creative industries: models of inter-disciplinary working can be found in the film studio, for example, with groups of different creative or artistic personnel such as set designers, foley artists, sound designers, composers, pre- and post-production editors, script writers, and many more, employed in the pursuit of a common artistic goal. New forms of technology have been employed within what might be seen as relatively conservative art forms such as ballet (for example, the TEEVE project[4] saw ballet dancers using video-conferencing technologies to develop collaborative approaches to dance in an online environment). Wherever we look, artists collaborate and, in many cases, technology helps inform and develop these collaborations in interesting ways.

Thirdly, from an educational perspective there is an argument that technology can act as a bridge between subject cultures. This is particularly true within the arts. John's metaphor of 'trading zones' (John 2005: 471) helpfully examines what he calls the 'borderlands' between subjects and technology, within which certain types of 'transaction' can take place. Using Galison's anthropological work as a starting point (Galison 1997), which in itself is an inter-disciplinary borrowing, John explores the various subject sub-cultures within physics, analysing the trading that takes place between theoreticians, experimentalists and engineers. He concludes:

> Exchanges between sub-cultures can be compared to the incomplete and partial relations which are established when different tribes come together for trading purposes. Each tribe can bring things to the 'trading space' and take things away; even sacred objects can be offered up and exchanged. This trading process also gives rise to new contact languages which are locally understood and co-ordinated. (John 2005: 485–486)

John suggests that the use of this 'trading zone' metaphor can help us understand more fully the transitory and evolving relationship between a subject culture and the technologies that are brought to bear upon it. The boundary between arts subjects and technology becomes permeable in such a model, with notions of success depending on the perceived value associated with the ideas presented, and the way in which the participants act upon these and understand them. John is anticipating an evolutionary space, one in which the every element becomes interdependent:

> 'Transaction spaces' are evolutionary where the affordances and constraints of the situation, the tools, and the setting can facilitate further interaction as well as limit it. To occupy a 'trading zone' does not mean abandoning one's 'sacred' disciplinary 'home' nor allowing the 'profane' to dominate the exchange; rather it respects subtle negotiation and accommodation (Wertsch 2003; Claxton et al., 2003) processes that encourage multiple and modified identities to emerge over time. (John 2005: 485-486)

REFLECTIVE TASK

This task explores how John's metaphor could be applied to your subject area, or a collection of subject areas (e.g. the performing arts). Consider the following questions drawn from his 'trading spaces' metaphor.

Reflective questions

1 What are the key things that your subject area can bring to the space to network and 'trade' with others?

2 Are there any particularly sacred objects within your subject that you can bring with you? How would you feel about these objects being shared within a network or traded and used by others?

3 New types of conversation or collaboration (in John's terms, 'contact languages') could emerge through this process of trading. What characteristics might these new languages have? Will others be able to understand these or will they remain localised?

4 What would the relationship be between my 'sacred home' and these new collaborative trading zones?

5 How can I ensure that any networking or trading is conducted in a sensitive and empathetic manner, ensuring the 'profane' does not dominate or exclude my conversations with others?

Our argument here is that technologically mediated exchanges or interactions of the type John anticipates are something that teachers could aspire to develop in their work. This is a key way in which connections can be built between our subjects. The Reflective Task asked you to consider what the 'sacred objects' within your subject culture might be. Is there willingness on your part to offer these up within such an exchange and allow them to be negotiated with or compromised? Cross-curricular, collaborative approaches that dominate education today seem to be dominated by low-value ('profane') exchanges. These are characterised by pieces of curriculum development that merge a subject down to its lowest common denominator, underplaying the well established strengths of its subject culture and replacing these with hastily constructed and meaningless uses of technology which disempower teachers and cut short the opportunities for their students' learning. In contrast, high-value exchanges will result in meaningful developments in arts education that centre on attributes that underpin ongoing teacher development. As John's conclusions assert:

> If this agenda is to materialise then schools and subjects need time to adjust to using ICT, to explore its possibilities and to engage with its affordances as well as understanding its constraints. Additionally, certain conditions need

to be prevalent if the further blending of technology and pedagogy within subjects is to flourish. These conditions are dependent on a number of characteristics, all of which, according to Eraut (2000), are regarded as fundamental to the creation of a suitable organisational microclimate. They include:

- A blame-free culture;

- Learning from experiences – positive and negative – at both group and individual levels;

- Trying to make full use of the various knowledge resources held by members;

- Encouraging talk about learning;

- Locating and using relevant knowledge from outside the group;

- Enhancing and extending understandings and capabilities of both the group as a whole and its individual members.

(John 2005: 484–485)

This advice is timely. New forms of networked teaching and learning, of the type we are promoting throughout this book, will depend on a communal sense of enquiry that is dominated by characteristics such as those John identifies.

Developing connections within subjects

There are many examples of how technology can be used to form new connections, ways of thinking and acting within specific subject areas. Keeping with the musical theme in the final part of this chapter, the following case study draws on the work of one experimental, improvising musician and composer whose work is particularly insightful. The case study, drawn from John Bowers' (2003) study 'Improvising Machines', explores the improvisation of electronic music from various standpoints, including its musicological, aesthetic, practical and technical-design dimensions. Within it, Bowers provides detailed ethnographic descriptions of his own musical performances over a number of years at different concerts across Europe. He describes how he uses various pieces of hardware and software through which these performances were facilitated. For anyone with an interest in technology, the human–design interface and the wider adoption of digital technologies within education, it is a fascinating account.

CASE STUDY: 'IMPROVISING MACHINES'

Electro-acoustic music is an indigenous 'machine music'. Bowers explores his own experience as an improviser in this idiom, giving special attention to observable variations in the forms of technical interactivity, social interaction and musical material which existed across the various musical performances that he gave with fellow performers. He identifies four key issues.

Contingent practical configurations

> The music has arisen in relation to these contingencies in such a way that, from an ethnographic point of view, it should not be analytically separated from them. (ibid: 43)

Bowers defines 'contingent practical configurations' as the technologies used, musical materials and forms explored, performance practices employed, and the specific setting and occasion of, as well as the understanding generated from, musical improvisation with technology. Contingencies of this type are 'topicalised' within the performance itself. They are integral to it and shape the resulting musical statements, interactions and expressions. Improvised musical conduct of the sort Bowers describes is a space in which contingencies are worked through in real time and in public. The specific contingency of a technology-rich musical improvisational conduct is embodied in the relationship between human beings and their machines. You can't have one without the other. Specifically, 'it is in our abilities to work with and display a manifold of human-machine relationships that our accountability of performance should reside' (ibid: 44).

Variable sociality

For Bowers, variable sociality is the different social interactions and relationships that are worked out through musical performance:

> The sociality of musical production is an important feature of improvised electro-acoustic music. Publicly displaying the different ways in which performers can position themselves with respect to each other and the different ways in which technologies can be deployed to enforce, negate, mesh with, disrupt, or otherwise relate to the local socialities of performance could [again] become the whole point of doing it. (ibid: 45)

As with any musical practice, within 'machine music' the social, interactional relationships that Bowers and his fellow musicians enjoyed varied over time. There was a deliberate playfulness. Different alternatives were experimented with, variably and often inter-changeably, within the course of a specific musical performance. Social norms could be disrupted at a particular point, perhaps due to technical issues (perhaps the cables were not long enough or the monitoring was lop-sided) or other factors (the audience began to leave or the music was too loud and complaints were received from others in the locality). The social dimensions of musical production are highly important. They need to be understood and explored as an integral part of the aesthetic, not as a separate issue.

Variable engagement and interactivity

Just as performers can variably relate to each other, they can variably engage with the technologies and instruments before them. (ibid: 45)

Linked to the above, Bowers' concept of variable engagement and interactivity facilitates a consideration of the different and varying relations that performers have with their instruments and technologies. In particular, he identifies a number of different patterns of engagement for the musical performer and for the listener.

His twelve-hour musical performance in Ipswich (at which audience members were given a free can of baked beans in return for their attendance) utilised a range of mechanised musical production technologies that, at particular points, automatically set new parameters for musical statements, or even drew on new source materials from the performers' laptop computers. The pattern of engagement from the performers' point of view was one of initiation, delegation, supervision and intervention. This process meant that it was not always necessary for one, or both, of the musical performers to be physically present within the space for the whole of the twelve hours.

Other more conventional forms of musical production within Bowers' performance events utilised conventional instruments that required some kind of human incitement to action (e.g. striking something or manually triggering a sample). The pattern of engagement here would be one of physical excitement/incitement and manipulation.

Different forms of engagement have different phenomenologies associated with them. How one listens, hears or responds intellectually or is physically moved all effect and affect one's engagement and interaction with sound and its means of production.

Musical materials

To construct workable and intelligible performance environments, I have made various distinctions between these musical materials in terms of their real-world sources, the media by which they are conveyed, the manipulability of those media, the kinds of gestures and devices which are used to realise those manipulations. From time to time, all of those features are seen to be bound up with identifiable forms of social organisation between co-performers, and those forms of interaction have musical-formal aspects to boot. I have tried to reveal these interconnections through ethnographic description of the performance situation. (ibid: 48)

Bowers' sophisticated organisation of musical materials draws on a range of existing methodological structures for electro-acoustic composition. Whilst he is at pains to emphasise the differences here, his account is illuminating when placed alongside his analysis of Schaeffer's acousmatic composition (and allied practices), Emmerson's distinction between aural and mimetic discourse, and Smalley's spectro-morphological categorisations. These all provide a frame for dialogue and discussion about the sounds that Bowers and his co-performers produced during their improvisations and, importantly for us, about how they reflected on and justified the musical 'product' that resulted at the various concerts.

Central to this discussion (ibid: 48–50) is the question of how an overall musical structure or 'syntax' can emerge from an improvised performance practice. Drawing directly on Emmerson's work on musical syntax (Emmerson 1986), Bowers writes:

> Improvised forms are naturally immanent, ad hoc-ed moment-by-moment on the basis of what has gone before and projecting opportunities for what might come following. In the language I hinted at above, multiple threads of significance may link up several of the elements in play. There may still be singularities and other 'unattached' offerings. The threads may be thin or may be densely interwoven (steady with the metaphor now!). We may have a sense of 'a piece' or a collection of 'moments' or some point in between. These are some of the immanent forms, of abstracted syntax, one can hear generated by electro-acoustic improvisors.
> (ibid: 50)

'Improvising Machines' presents an illuminating and sophisticated narrative about the processes and products of a musician's improvisational conduct within the context of electro-acoustic music. It contains a blend of musicological features, technical considerations and reflective comments, underpinned throughout by a rigorous approach to ethnographic and critical analysis. What can it teach us about a networked approach to education and how such an approach could be enriched through the use of technology?

All education takes place within a rich context of contingent practical elements

The contingent practical context of education in schools is fundamental and integral to any networked approach to teaching and learning. It is only through a strong commitment to exploring the intricate relationships that develop that a true (or at least defensible) understanding of what education with these technologies really is can be created.

This raises a number of pertinent questions. To what extent are you able to map out the contingent practical elements at work within a particular context or process of instruction within or beyond your classroom? The type and location of these elements might be diverse, extending from the classroom where learning might be initiated to to the students' home environment where it continues and develops; from conversations with their friends at school to conversations they have online with others about their work. They may include formal elements, such as the unit of work within which the learning is contextualised, and informal elements, such as the computer game that the student played yesterday. They will undoubtedly include the quality of relationship the student has with their teacher, their peers, other family members and other admired role models. They will also include a whole range of digital technologies.

Understanding these elements is important if we are to truly understand and know how that student's learning has developed. Only through developing a rich understanding of the broad network within which that student's work has been produced will you begin to understand why they have made their particular choices.

Education always takes place within a rich technological context

Technologies are integral to all education. They can help enforce the social order, or they can negate it; they can facilitate a meshing of ideas and responses, or they may helpfully or unhelpfully disrupt them. We have seen this on many occasions throughout our book. The rich technological context of our students' lives today impacts fundamentally on their use in educational settings. The broad array of technology that mediates our students' lives implicates, fundamentally, their engagement with us as teachers, and their education more broadly. We cannot escape this, but we need to understand it. We hope this book has provided some clear frameworks within which you can understand these things more fully.

Working productively with technologies: initiation, delegation, supervision and intervention

As Bowers' work demonstrates, using technology is a complex business. It builds on numerous contingent practical elements and configurations that are mediated through a process of variable sociality. It demands that we are able to diagnose and work within a range of approaches in an integrated and holistic way. Trying to disassemble skills, concepts or processes as technological or non-technological is nonsensical. As teachers, it is vital that we understand these processes, and that policy-makers develop examination and accountability frameworks that facilitate them in an integrated way.

Different technologies demand different approaches. We need to encourage our students to be flexible; to embrace and respond, intuitively and fluently, to the emerging forms of engagement that these technologies demand. As teachers, we can initiate something. We can start our students off in a direction. But following an initiation, there is a delegation. For effective learning to take place, we need to allow our students to take ownership of their ideas. They need space and autonomy, time to explore, to experiment, to work with their machines and obtain outcomes that are of value to them. Delegation might involve handing over significant control to a technology, for a time, to see what emerges. The key here is to consider the human endeavour in equal measure to the technological input. It is the student who will add value to a technological utterance within their learning network.

If students are not to continue their work indefinitely, there will come a time when the teacher has to exercise a legitimate supervisory role. Perhaps the time is up for that piece of work, a new direction needs to be taken, or the deadline for submission is near. With supervision comes intervention. Intervention might mean a day of reckoning, a formal assessment or examination. However, it could just mean a moment of reckoning or accountability, a pointing in a new direction – a tack as it were – before the students are off again.

Initiation, delegation, supervision and intervention; here is just one potential approach to a networked education that is in tune with the ways of working with digital technologies inspired by Bowers' 'Improvising Machines'.

In addition to all this, Bowers' work demonstrates the importance of engaging fully with the process of seeking to understand how technology mediates our work. As teachers, it is vital that we commit to this process fully and do not leave it to others. Our conceptual and pedagogical models for education and how it is organised must be built on an understanding that embraces technology, of any shape and form, and sees it as integral to the teaching and learning activities that we plan. Technology is too important and too prevalent to be categorised as being solely within the domain of some 'experts' and left at the doorstep of others.

Using social media to form new partnerships

In the short story *Cipher in the Snow* (Todhunter 1982), Cliff Evans gets off the bus one day in the middle of winter, stumbles onto the pavement and dies, suddenly, in a snowbank. His teacher is asked to write his obituary. He struggles to find anyone in the staffroom who had exchanged more than two words with the boy during the academic year. Not even ten students from the school had known Cliff well enough to go to his funeral. The teacher resolves never to allow another student in his class to become a zero, a cipher. No students in the future will ever be so unconnected, so unknown, that they just unconnect from life itself.

The story is a valuable parable, reminding us of something that we all spend a great deal of time on in the first few weeks of a new term but which, perhaps, we may be less than diligent in continuing throughout the academic year. Picture your classroom space. There are doubtless many connections there. Now think of the number of connections that the students are not making because of existing social relations, class arrangements or architecture. How many of those who sit next to each other know each other's names, or where they have lived during the past five years, or what their families do on holidays?

How can we rethink the classroom as providing an endless stream of meaningful connection? How can we break out of the four walls of that classroom, defy the architecture and even the physical geography of our institutions to forge the connections that will have a dramatic effect on our students' learning? Here are some practical ideas to help you develop a new classroom by connecting.

■ Do a project blog with another class. Have a weekly Twitter chat with another class.

■ Change the layout of the room you're using. If there is a single focus (all the students facing forward to a particular point) change it: have multiple focus points. Do you really need seats to discuss ideas? Find ways of encouraging side conversations – everything doesn't have to be 'on-task'. So much of what we learn happens at the periphery of the tasks we aim to complete. Allow for serendipity. If the overall objective is met, allow flexible routes to achieving it.

■ Introduce your students to Global Voices[5] and then ask every student to start, develop and maintain a serious blog site. There are many ways that this can be achieved effectively, at no financial cost and within the safeguards for privacy and safety. This will give all students an audience and connect them to others. They'll learn how to write online, and how to recognise and evaluate information online. Feed your students' blogs into a curation blog (using RSS feed aggregators – the plugin FeedWordPress[6] works well for this, or use a magazine-style feed reader such as Feedly). Publicise the address around your school and with parents. Encourage everyone to comment.

■ Use Twitter to build relationships with parents. Tweetpic classroom learning activities. Tweet questions to stimulate conversation between parents and children on the learning they have been doing. Think of the technology as enabling a three-way conversation between students, teachers and parents. Allay fears of social media by talking about them, discussing the advantages and explaining the safeguards you use.

■ Use Skype[7] in the classroom to connect with a class in another country. Use it to practise a language your students are learning, or to find out about a town/country from a group of students who are living there.

■ Find a European teacher and school to connect with via eTwinning,[8] European Schoolnet's portal for schools wanting to find partners, resources, advice and help. Find out what teachers in the UK are saying about eTwinning on its YouTube channel.[9]

■ Join The Global Read Aloud.[10] This site coordinates the activities of a six-week read-a-book-aloud period where as many connections as possible are made over this one book. It's been going three years and has forged more than 200,000 connections.

■ Use the British Council SchoolsOnline partner-finding tool.[11] With 40,000 teachers registered in 180 countries, it's very easy to begin connecting your classroom to the world outside.

Summary

This chapter has explored two key themes. We explored the pedagogical implications of a networked approach to teaching and learning. Specifically, we considered how knowledge can be transformed through the tools and techniques associated with a networked approach. We considered a range of teaching styles and roles, and explored what these might look like in your classroom. We have also considered how the key messages of our book impact on the partnerships that you might form within your teaching. Beginning with traditional approaches to partnership, we have extended our thinking both across and within subjects, and urged you to commit to understanding the impact that technology, especially social media, can play in developing new educational approaches.

At the heart of all of this is you, the teacher. Teaching is all about relationships. The key relationship is, of course, between you and an individual student. As any counsellor will tell you, in order to understand someone else you have understand yourself. This is why so many courses of initial teacher education begin with a process of self-realisation of some sort.

Using social media and other technologies within a connectivist approach to teaching and learning will take time to develop. It will be unsettling at times and we guess, at certain points, you will wonder whether it is worth continuing. It is! However, the most important thing is to 'walk the walk' as well as 'talk the talk'. Being an example of this approach will teach your students a lot more than trying to incorporate a specific activity or example in a lesson plan. So, finally in this chapter, here are some things you can share with others and with the world – and they won't cost you anything.

- Make your opinion heard. Help a cause through Change.org[12] or amplify your voice by using Thunderclap,[13] which enables you to share a cause or event in mass, flash-mob style via Facebook, Twitter or Tumblr.

- Give your time. Volunteermatch[14] will help you find opportunities to volunteer that relate to your personal interests.

- Be more generous than is absolutely necessary. Watch Life Vest Inside[15] to get inspired about the way kindness spreads.

- Give a better planet to future generations – pick up litter. Post your finds on Instagram Literati,[16] which identifies what type of rubbish is gathering where.

- Give blood. Join the largest network linking blood donation to hospitals and blood banks at Socialblood.[17]

- Take Charity Miles[18] with you when you cycle, walk or run. The miles you cover will be converted into money for your choice of worthy causes included on the platform.

Notes

1 www.spigot.org
2 Royal Society for the encouragement of Arts, Manufactures and Commerce, www.thersa.org
3 Now Aldeburgh Music; see www.aldeburgh.co.uk
4 Tele-immersive Environment for EVErybody, cairo.cs.uiuc.edu/projects/teleimmersion
5 globalvoicesonline.org
6 wordpress.org/plugins/feedwordpress
7 education.skype.com
8 www.etwinning.net
9 www.youtube.com/user/eTwinning
10 www.globalreadaloud.com
11 schoolsonline.britishcouncil.org/partner-with-a-school
12 www.change.org
13 www.thunderclap.it/en
14 www.volunteermatch.org
15 www.lifevestinside.com
16 www.litterati.org
17 socialblood.org
18 www.charitymiles.org

References

Bowers, J. (2003). 'Improvising Machines'. cid.nada.kth.se/pdf/CID-195.pdf [last accessed 1/2/15].

Claxton, G., Pollard, A. and Sutherland, R. (2003). 'Fishing in the fog: conceptualising learning at the confluence of cultures', in Sutherland, R., Claxton, G. and Pollard, A. (eds), *Learning and Teaching: Where world views meet*. Stoke on Trent, Trentham Books.

Downes, S. (2010). 'The Role of the Educator' *The Huffington Post* June 12. www.huffingtonpost.com/stephen-downes/the-role-of-the-educator_b_790973.html [last accessed 14/6/2014]

Emmerson, S. (1986). 'The relation of language to materials', in Emmerson, S. (ed.), *The Language of Electroacoustic Music*. London, Methuen.

Eraut, M. (2000). 'Non-formal learning and tacit knowledge in professional work'. *British Journal of Educational Psychology* 70 (1), 113–136.

Galison, P. (1997). *Image and Logic: The material culture of micro-physics*. Chicago, IL, University of Chicago Press.

Higham, J. and Yeomans, D. (2009). 'Working together? Partnership approaches to 14–19 education in England'. *British Educational Research Journal* 36, 1–23.

Jarche, H. (2010). 'Network Learning: Working Smarter with PKM'. www.jarche.com/2010/10/network-learning-working-smarter [last accessed 2/8/14].

John, P. (2005). The sacred and the profane: subject sub-culture, pedagogical practice and teachers' perceptions of the classroom uses of ICT'. *Educational Review* 57 (4): 469–488.

Kanter, B. (2014). 'Content Curation Primer'. www.bethkanter.org/content-curation-101 [last accessed 2/8/14].

Kushner, S. (1999). 'Fringe benefits: music education out of the National Curriculum'. *Music Education Research* 1 (2): 209–218.

Mosston, M. and Ashworth, S. (2002). *Teaching Physical Education* (5th edn). San Francisco, CA, B. Cummings.

RSA (2009). *Towards an Area Based Curriculum: Insights and directions from the research*. London, RSA (Royal Society for the encouragement of Arts, Manufactures and Commerce).

RSA (2012). *Thinking About an Area-Based Curriculum: A guide for practitioners.* London, RSA (Royal Society for the encouragement of Arts, Manufactures and Commerce).

Savage, J. and Challis, M. (2002). 'Electroacoustic composition: practical models of composition with new technologies'. *Journal of the Sonic Arts Network* 14, 8–13.

Savage, J. and Fautley, M. (2010). *Cross Curricular Teaching and Learning in the Secondary School: The arts.* London, Routledge.

Scoble, R. (2010). 'The Seven Needs of Real-time Curators'. scobleizer.com/?p=6373 [last accessed 22/7/14].

Seltzer, K. and Bentley, T. (1999). *The Creative Age: Knowledge and skills for the new economy.* London, Demos.

Siemens, G. (2005). 'Connectivism: A Learning Theory for the Digital Age'. www.itdl.org/journal/jan_05/article01.htm [last accessed 1/2/15].

Swanwick, K. and Lawson, D. (1999). 'Authentic music and its effect on the attitudes and musical development of secondary school pupils'. *Music Education Research* 1 (1): 47–60.

Thomson, P. (2002). *Schooling the Rustbelt Kids: Making the difference in changing times.* Stoke on Trent, UK, Trentham Books.

Todhunter, J. M. (1982). *Cipher in the Snow.* Newport Beach, CA, KenningHouse.

Weisgerber, C. (2014). 'Building Thought Leadership through Content Curation'. www.slideshare.net/corinnew/building-thought-leadership-through-content-curation [last accessed 4/8/14].

Wertsch, J. (2003). 'Dimensions of culture-clash', in Sutherland, R., Claxton, G. and Pollard, A. (eds), *Learning and Teaching: Where world views meet.* Stoke on Trent, UK, Trentham Books.

5 You are not a gadget[1]

KEY QUESTIONS

- What are the limits of technology's use in education?
- What, if anything, are we losing as technology's influence on education increases?
- What can I, or should I, do about it?

The cult of educational technology

In *To Save Everything, Click Here*, Evgeny Morozov (2013) looks at two discourses that have permeated the technology industry, and through it our own lives and government policy over the past ten years. One is 'internet-centrism', the tendency to look at the internet as the technological structure and inevitable master narrative that will shape the future of all our institutions and social practices. The second is 'technological solutionism', the strategy of jumping onto simple technological solutions to problems before knowing exactly what those problems are, and how they might be framed and understood.

Morozov does not write directly about education in his book, but it is not difficult to extrapolate some of his arguments. One story we have told in this book is that the model of education as conceived in the era of industrial mass production is giving way to another, less top-down, more participatory, networked model where knowledge is created through the connections we make. Clearly this is a journey that is going to take some time. Whilst writing this chapter, we noted the headmaster at Eton College has been complaining about the examination system within the United Kingdom. He believes that an exam system that 'obliges students to sit alone at their desks in preparation for a world in which, for much of the time, they will need to work collaboratively' is one that is failing (Ratcliffe 2014). There is much work to be done, at many levels.

Some interpretations of the story we have told throughout this book have been simplified and distorted to read thus:

- The web has changed everything;

- Education is dying, therefore ...

- We need more technology to fix education.

This is what Morozov means when he talks about 'internet solutionism'. Clearly, it is a danger. As we have seen, technology is not neutral. It changes what we are able to see (think of how astronomy changed with the invention of the telescope) and privileges certain types of behaviour. However, in thinking it is the solution without working on the problem, we fall into a trap. If you think the current model of education is 'dying', the reasons are likely to be very complex and susceptible to various interpretations. Those need to be found and debated before any simple fix is applied. Sadly, within the educational world generally this seldom happens and, as we will see in the examples below, inappropriate uses of technology can often make the problem worse rather than better.

What are the consequences of this loss for our work as educators?

The rise of the quick fix

Morozov's work is also helpful in thinking about the massive amounts of data about learning and teaching currently being collected through online learning networks. One example is the Khan Academy.[2] This web phenomenon provides students with free access to thousands of video lectures that describe key processes in many subjects. Want to learn how to do long division? Want to know what photosynthesis is? Want to calculate how many atoms are in one mole of gold? There are videos to help you learn how to do all of this. However, the Khan Academy is not a substitute for a coherent curriculum in mathematics, biology or chemistry. It is also not a substitute for a real teacher. It is not a complete educational resource in any meaningful sense because it was not designed to be that in the first place. Robert Talbert put it like this on his blog:

> When we say that someone has 'learned' a subject, we typically mean that they have shown evidence of mastery not only of basic cognitive processes like factual recall and working mechanical exercises but also higher-level tasks like applying concepts to new problems and judging between two equivalent concepts. A student learning calculus, for instance, needs to demonstrate that s/he can do things like take derivatives of polynomials and use the Chain Rule. But if this is all they can demonstrate, then it's stretching it to say that the student has 'learned calculus', because calculus is a lot more than just executing mechanical processes correctly and quickly. To say that it is not – that knowledge of calculus consists in the ability to perform algorithmic processes quickly and accurately – is to adopt an impoverished definition of the subject that renders a great intellectual pursuit into a collection of party tricks. [...]

Khan Academy is great for learning about lots of different subjects. But it's not really adequate for learning those subjects on a level that really makes a difference in the world. Learning at these levels requires more than watching videos (or lectures) and doing exercises. It takes hard work (by both the learner and the instructor), difficult assignments that get students to work at these higher levels, open channels of communication that do not just go one way, and above all a **relationship between learner and instructor that engenders trust**. (Talbert 2012; our emphasis)

Please remember this key point about trust. We return to it later in this chapter.

Losing our humanity

But there is another problem here. The Khan Academy and other adaptive systems that claim to personalise learning rely on algorithms that use data produced by the students who are using the systems. These mathematical systems claim to increase efficiency and measure improvement. However, they can only express themselves in mathematical terms. Therefore, Morozov argues, these educational systems sacrifice what he calls 'narrative imagination' for 'numeric imagination'. In other words, in a desperate attempt to quantify our students' attainment and progress, we are losing the ability to express the rich tapestry of what it means to be human, of what it means to learn.

There is a significant strain among more sceptically inclined writers about the role of technology in society that resonates with Morozov's writings. Sherry Turkle looks at exactly the problem of what it means to be human in her book *Alone Together* (Turkle 2011). She does so by examining the irony that in a world where young people have never been so connected, there is more loneliness than ever before. She also examines the consequences of arriving at what she calls the 'robotic moment' where we are delegating more and more of our interactions to robots through technology. She has researched this for many years in various locations, including the use of robotic toys for children, immersive online environments such as Second Life, and the adoption of technological gadgets to 'care' for elderly folk in residential homes. Rather than being in the world and interacting with it and the people around us, her book documents a mediated world, one that we interact with through screens. In her conclusion, she describes the narrative of her study as an arc:

We expect more from technology and less from each other. This puts us at the still center of a perfect storm. Overwhelmed, we have been drawn to connections that seem low risk and always at hand: Facebook friends, avatars, IRC chat partners. If convenience and control continue to be our priorities, we shall be tempted by sociable robots, where, like gamblers at their slot machines, we are promised excitement programmed in, just enough to keep us in the game. At the robotic moment, we have to be concerned that the simplification and reduction of relationship is no longer something we complain about. It may become what we expect, even desire. (Turkle 2011: 295)

As with Morozov, who argues that we are losing the 'narrative imagination', Turkle suggests that in increasingly defaulting to the digital (by which she means text messages, Facebook updates, Skype meetings and the like) we are losing the raw human part of what it means to be with each other.

The dying art of conversation

We were sitting in a restaurant, trying to have a conversation, but her children, 4-year-old Willow and 7-year-old Luca, would not stop fighting. The arguments – over a fork, or who had more water in a glass – were unrelenting. Like a magician quieting a group of children by pulling a rabbit out of a hat, my sister reached into her purse and produced two shiny Apple iPads, handing one to each child. Suddenly, the two were quiet. Eerily so. They sat playing games and watching videos, and we continued with our conversation. After our meal, as we stuffed the iPads back into their magic storage bag, my sister felt slightly guilty. 'I don't want to give them the iPads at the dinner table, but if it keeps them occupied for an hour so we can eat in peace, and more importantly not disturb other people in the restaurant, I often just hand it over,' she told me. Then she asked: 'Do you think it's bad for them? I do worry that it is setting them up to think it's OK to use electronics at the dinner table in the future.' I did not have an answer, and although some people might have opinions, no one has a true scientific understanding of what the future might hold for a generation raised on portable screens. (Bilton 2013)

What did you make of this story? As parents, we can relate to the parents in this story and the pressures facing us in the context of dealing with noisy children in a restaurant. However, what are the down sides here? Are there other ways that this could have been dealt with? And does it really matter?

One of the areas that digital sceptics have identified in recent years has been around the dying art of conversation. Sherry Turkle, whose work we discussed above, is so worried about this that her new book, to be published in autumn 2015, will be called *Reclaiming Conversation*. She was interviewed about this book for *The Atlantic* early in 2014:

[It's] not, technically, that we're not talking to each other. We're talking all the time, in person as well as in texts, in e-mails, over the phone, on Facebook and Twitter. The world is more talkative now, in many ways, than it's ever been. The problem, Turkle argues, is that all of this talk can come at the expense of conversation. We're talking at each other rather than with each other. [...] Conversations, as they tend to play out in person, are messy – full of pauses and interruptions and topic changes and assorted awkwardness. But the messiness is what allows for true exchange. It gives participants the time – and, just as important, the permission – to think and react and glean insights. 'You can't always tell, in a conversation, when the interesting bit is going to come', Turkle says. 'It's like dancing: slow, slow, *quick-quick*, slow. You know? It seems boring, but all of a sudden there's something, and *whoa*.' (Garber 2014)

Might it be that our students, albeit hyper-connected, have simply never learned how to hold conversations? To illustrate this, here is a case study drawn from the work of one teacher (Barnwell 2014).

MY STUDENTS DON'T KNOW HOW TO HAVE A CONVERSATION

Recently I stood in front of my class, observing an all-too-familiar scene. Most of my students were covertly – or so they thought – pecking away at their smartphones under their desks, checking their Facebook feeds and texts. As I called their attention, students' heads slowly lifted, their eyes reluctantly glancing forward. I then cheerfully explained that their next project would practice a skill they all desperately needed: holding a conversation.

Several students looked perplexed. Others fidgeted in their seats, waiting for me to stop watching the class so they could return to their phones. Finally, one student raised his hand. 'How is this going to work?' he asked.

My junior English class had spent time researching different education issues. We had held whole-class discussions surrounding school reform issues and also practiced one-on-one discussions. Next, they would create podcasts in small groups, demonstrating their ability to communicate about the topics – the project represented a culminating assessment of their ability to speak about the issues in real time.

Even with plenty of practice, the task proved daunting to students. I watched trial runs of their podcasts frequently fall silent. Unless the student facilitator asked a question, most kids were unable to converse effectively. Instead of chiming in or following up on comments, they conducted rigid interviews. They shuffled papers and looked down at their hands. Some even reached for their phones – an automatic impulse and the last thing they should be doing.

As I watched my class struggle, I came to realise that conversational competence might be the single most overlooked skill we fail to teach students. Kids spend hours each day engaging with ideas and one another through screens – but rarely do they have an opportunity to truly hone their interpersonal communication skills. Admittedly, teenage awkwardness and nerves play a role in difficult conversations. But students' reliance on screens for communication is detracting – and distracting – from their engagement in real-time talk.

It might sound like a funny question, but we need to ask ourselves: Is there any 21st-century skill more important than being able to sustain confident, coherent conversation? (Barnwell 2014)

Is this something you recognise in your own work as a teacher? If you are a more experienced teacher, is it something you have noticed changing over recent years?

The (lack of) joy in learning

Learning management systems such as Moodle[3] and WebCT (Blackboard)[4] are pervasive across schools, colleges and universities. For many of us working within these institutions, they have been seen as the answer to a whole range of problems. In the past year I have heard about Moodle being used within my university to solve problems of limited face-to-face contact time with undergraduate students (due to a new timetabling system); to help the university fulfil its green agenda by becoming a paperless academic environment; to support the marking of work electronically within a four-week turn-around period; and to encourage more collaboration between students within units of work via online forums.

It is very hard to find critics of such an approach. But we would argue that centralised learning management systems like Moodle are an imposition on the structures of teaching and learning, and nearly always are more harmful than beneficial. Why?

They are principally about management and not learning

Think of the language in the term 'learning management system'. 'Learning' is fine. This is what we have been talking about throughout this book. What we have not been talking about is the framing of learning as something to 'manage' with 'systems' established to do the management. Those people who have developed learning management systems, and those who implement them, however, have been thinking about management. The result is a piece of software that is concerned with how to manage 'users', how to define and standardise the roles they are able to play, and how to ensure user privileges are allocated on a top-down basis. It is hardly surprising that the resulting environment for learning is dull, routine and rigid. Just ask any university student. We suspect the same is true for your students.

They are closed systems

Learning management system software presents a closed system that does not easily encourage interaction with the wider web or other repositories of public knowledge. Formal education that closes learning in this way can hardly claim to be engaging with the community or contributing to the stock of public knowledge. Learning management systems are as much about exclusion as they are about inclusion. The walled-garden principle of these systems may by-pass issues of student privacy and keep ethics statements simple, but they offer little longer-lasting education about what learning really looks like in the world. Once students leave the 'system', the university or school, they are precluded from taking part in the 'system' any further. This is a narrative of separation.

They serve the interests of the management and not the learner

Learning management systems make a mockery of the idea of student-centred, life-long learning. They are lock-step management systems that, like the curricula they inscribe, process students towards an exit point. While the student exits, the learning that did take place, those forum conversations and assignments submitted, stays in the system as data to inform its next iteration. The student takes nothing away.

They de-skill students

The hours spent in environments within learning management systems rarely teach our students the kinds of digital literacy skills that they might expect to be useful as they continue to learn outside formal schooling and move into work. Yes, they learn to navigate the system, read the notes, watch the videos and presentation slides, but rarely do they participate as producers of knowledge, and rarely are they able to share what they learn and teach others what they know. In our university, there is often great talk about 'employability' and 'transferable skills', yet the very platform for institutional learning has been designed in such a way as to mitigate against these things.

They are inflexible and depersonalise learning

Because the running and maintenance of such systems is increasingly outsourced (learning is conceptualised as an administrative cost that can be reduced by efficiency savings), the opportunities for making the systems more flexible to a student's personal requirements are lost. They are what they are, and there are minimal, if any, opportunities to make personal changes. Make no mistake here, learning management systems are extraordinarily complex and vast systems with, at least where we work, large numbers of people relying on them twenty-four hours a day, 365 days a year. As they are so big, so all encompassing, there is little enthusiasm for creating learning environments that cannot be incorporated into them. The peripheral projects, the test-sites and the experiments are invariably seen either as in competition with learning management systems or as something that should be absorbed by them.

They limit interaction

Above all, learning management systems do not let learners connect beyond their prescribed cohort, which has been administratively assigned to their virtual learning area. Opportunities for collaboration are closed down. Cross-disciplinary work is proscribed. Inter-university cooperation is made difficult. All those connections between learners and their environment are, in effect, severed by a system designed to manage, not promote, learning.

Constant distraction

The iPad is the new must-have 'educational' gadget. We often joke that it's difficult to move in the many schools we visit across the north-west of England due to the stacks of iPads (other tablets are available) that have been bought by head-teachers anxious for their next technological fix. For us, the iPad is simply another learning management system, closed and top-down. The model of interaction that the iPad represents puts the student fair and square in the role of consumer, a consumer who does not need to know anything about the 'device'. In one sense, of course, there is nothing to know. When you need a professional to change the batteries of an iPad, there's something wrong. The Maker movement's dictum, 'if you can't open it, don't own it', should be read as a warning here. This is system control, enabling privileges to mix and modify, to the lucky few. The politburo of such a system lies in the iTunes store. You might be able to make an app, but you can't distribute it without permission; you can't distribute it to work on different platforms. Just like students in a learning management system, you are locked in.

More generally, some educators are beginning to ask whether students really need to spend more time staring at screens as part of their formal schooling. As we have seen already, many writers are expressing increasing reservations about the impact of mobile and social technologies and the detrimental effects they have on our lives. Mark Bauerlein's *The Dumbest Generation* (2008) presents a compelling alternative that we would be wise to consider. In his wonderful blog on this book, Peter Lawler asks the question about whether this might be both the smartest and dumbest generation that has ever existed. Through twelve provocative points, he amplifies Bauerlein's thesis in a highly entertaining way.

1   Virtually all of our students have hours – and often many, many hours – of daily exposure to screens.

2   So they excel at multitasking and interactivity, and they have very strong spatial skills.

3   They also have remarkable visual acuity; they're ready for rushing images and updated information.

4   But these skills don't transfer well to – they don't have much to do with – the non-screen portions of their lives.

5   Their screen experiences, in fact, undermine their taste and capacity for building knowledge and developing their verbal skills.

6   They, for example, hate quiet and being alone. Because they rely so much on screens keeping them connected, they can't rely on themselves. Because they're constantly restless or stimulated, they don't know what it is to enjoy civilized leisure. The best possible punishment for an adolescent today is to make him or her spend an evening alone in his or her room without any screens, devices, or gadgets to divert him or her. It's amazing the extent to which screens have become multidimensional diversions from what we really know about ourselves.

7   Young people today typically are too agitated and impatient to engage in concerted study. Their imaginations are impoverished when they're visually unstimulated. So their *eros* is too. They can't experience anxiety as a prelude to wonder, and they too rarely become seekers and searchers.

8   They have trouble comprehending or being moved by the linear, sequential analysis of texts.

9   So they find it virtually impossible to spend an idle afternoon with a detective story and nothing more.

10 That's why they can be both so mentally agile and culturally ignorant. That's even why they know little to nothing about how to live well with love and death, as well as why their relational lives are so impoverished.

11 And that's why higher education – or liberal education – has to be about giving students experiences that they can't get on screen. That's even why liberal education has to have as little as possible to do with screens.

12 Everywhere and at all times, liberal education is countercultural. And so today it's necessarily somewhat anti-technology, especially anti-screen. That's one reason among many I'm so hard on MOOCs, online courses, PowerPoint, and anyone who uses the word 'disrupting' without subversive irony.

(Lawler 2013)

We like that Lawler highlights, simultaneously, the potential affordances and limitations of screens and the experiences that they present. However, we are also sure that there is much here that you will agree and disagree with. For us, though, point 11 is telling and we agree entirely with him on this. Higher education, liberal education, in fact any education must be about giving students experiences that they cannot get on screen, not just seek to replicate things on screens in insipid ways.

In the field of digital technologies, we need to be very critical about the affordances and limitations they offer for education. Here, as much as anywhere, using the principles of mediated action can help us gain a more detailed understanding of these powerful tools and the contexts within which we want to use them.

What does education really need?

The first half of this chapter has provided a more sceptical tone about the rise of technology in education. There are strong arguments that centre around Morozov's concept of 'internet solutionism' that suggest that we, as a society, have prioritised quick fixes rather than longer-term, meaningful solutions to our problems; that we have lost key elements of what it means to be together as human beings; that the art of conversation is dying; that learning has become overly managed in systems that squeeze the joy of learning to the point of extinction; and that many of us are constantly distracted by mobile and screen-based technologies. Hardly a cheerful picture! And, of course, it begs a question. What should our response be as teachers?

Skilful teachers

Firstly, and most importantly, our educational system needs skilful teachers. We firmly believe that teaching is built on a professional relationship between teacher and student. There is nothing that technology offers at the moment that can better the one-to-one human interaction between a skilful teacher and their student.

To be a skilful teacher, you have to develop a skilful pedagogy. This will take time, a commitment to regular evaluation and reflection (of which more in Chapter 6), and a willingness to work collaboratively with others. This pedagogy is built on many different components, intrinsically linked to you, your personality and character, and your understanding of your subject area(s) and your broader experiences.

Teaching is by nature a creative activity. In Chapter 1 we explored a range of definitions of creativity. Key words that we considered there included originality, imagination, exploration, discovering, creating and communicating. All of these, and so much more, can be used to describe the work of the skilful teacher.

Good teachers know that the ideas and content within their individual lessons, units of work and broader curricular frameworks are part of that wider network of concepts and ideas that frame our work. They are able to contextualise knowledge, skill and understanding within carefully crafted educational activities and then sequence these together to promote their students' learning.

At the end of the day, the teacher–student relationship is one that is built on trust. This is the very thing that it is hard to replicate through technology. There will always be a role for skilful teachers.

Great communicators

In his classic book on pedagogy (Alexander 2008), Robin Alexander describes Douglas Brown, an inspirational and exceptional teacher at the Perse School in Cambridge during the 1950s. Perhaps not surprisingly, the teaching of Brown that Alexander describes is very different from that which many teachers provide today.

For example, Alexander reflects on the way Brown talked to his classes (ibid: 156) in a way that today would be considered a monologue. But Alexander explores Brown's intellectual, moral and pedagogical approaches which resulted, he says, in a display of the 'humility of genius and the artistry of teaching' at their best. The broad pedagogical approach Brown adopted led Alexander to describe him as not one teacher but four (language, literature, music, and the man through whom the power of these was unlocked).

It is notable that Alexander chooses to describe him as 'not one teacher but four', rather than 'not one teacher but three'. Brown's sense of personality and identity informed his teaching in powerful ways. The greatest subject that Brown taught was life itself. Within his English classes, individual subjects were subsumed through a skilful educational dialogue between teacher and pupil that we would be wise to try and recapture in our schools today.

We were reminded of Douglas Brown whilst we were writing the case study and surrounding text about the 'death' of conversation. Clearly, we do not think that conversation and verbal communication is completely absent from our students' lives. As has been pointed out throughout this book, communication can take many forms, and it would be churlish to bemoan what might be considered a broadening or rebalancing of communication methods in our digital age.

But in another sense, the art of the teacher's voice has been diminished in recent years. Teacher talk is something that is often unhelpfully frowned upon. In their teacher training programmes, young teachers are often told not to speak for too long at any one time. Why? Students get bored and distracted. Yet the obvious response here is that teachers should be taught to talk well. When it is done well, students would be engaged and motivated. We too easily succumb to a narrative that says the richest form of communication we have at our disposal, our spoken language, should be limited in use and minimised in impact. We need to rediscover the art of great, engaging, spoken communication in our teaching.

Clear boundaries

When we are at our best, thinking about technology brings us back to questions about what really matters. When I recently travelled to a memorial service for a close friend, the program, on heavy cream-colored card stock, listed the afternoon's speakers, told who would play what music, and displayed photographs of my friend as a young woman and in her prime. Several around me used the program's stiff, protective wings to hide their cell phones as they sent text messages during the service. One of the texting mourners, a woman in her late sixties, came over to chat with me after the service. Matter-of-factly, she offered, 'I couldn't stand to sit that long without getting on my phone.' The point of the service was to take a moment. This woman had been schooled by a technology she'd had for less than a decade to find this close to impossible. (Turkle 2011: 295–296)

What is your response to this story? Is it too late to address some of the more overwhelming and potential addictive personality traits that such technologies place on us as individuals, and the resulting unhelpful negative affordances within our educational systems? Turkle thinks not. She describes a crisis or, in her phrase, a 'point of inflection' where we can see the potential costs of such a technological revolution and need to engage with it productively:

> We can start to take action. We will begin with very simple things. Some will seem like just reclaiming good manners. Talk to colleagues down the hall, no cell phones at dinner, on the playground, in the car, or in company. There will be more complicated things: to name only one, nascent efforts to reclaim privacy would be supported across the generations. And compassion is due to those of us – and there are many of us – who are so dependent on our devices that we cannot sit still for a funeral service or a lecture or a play. We now know that our brains are rewired every time we use a phone to search or surf or multitask. As we try to reclaim our concentration, we are literally at war with ourselves. Yet, no matter how difficult, it is time to look again toward the virtues of solitude, deliberateness, and living fully in the moment. [...] We deserve better. When we remind ourselves that it is we who decide how to keep technology busy, we shall have better. (Turkle 2011: 296)

Teachers and school leaders need to create clear boundaries for the use and application of technology. This will, we believe, almost certainly result in spaces where technology is not used as part of routine teaching and learning. In other spaces, and for other purposes, the full force of social media and other technologies should be embraced for educational purposes.

The key point here is that decisions need to be taken, and these decisions need to be informed by, supported with, and justified through a full understanding of the potential affordances and limitations of any technology. Remember Morozov's concept of 'technological solutionism' that we introduced at the beginning of this chapter. This is the trait of jumping onto simple technological solutions to problems before knowing exactly what those problems are, and how they might be framed and understood. Technological solutionism should have no place in our educational institutions. Here, more than anywhere else, we believe, educators should take time and develop the wisdom to get these decisions right first time. Our students are too important to be experimented on as a result of shoddy decision making.

We should also remember that there are some things in education that technology should not do. Here is one example:

> Edexcel, the largest educational testing firm in England, had announced it was introducing 'artificial intelligence-based, automated marking of exam essays'. The computerized grading system would 'read and assess' the essays that British students write as part of a widely used test of language proficiency. A spokesman for Edexcel, which is a subsidiary of the media conglomerate

Pearson, explained that the system 'produced the accuracy of human markers while eliminating human elements such as tiredness and subjectivity,' according to a report in the *Times Educational Supplement*. A testing expert told the paper that the computerized evaluation of essays would be a mainstay of education in the future: 'the uncertainty is "when" not "if"'. (Carr 2010: 223)

Does this story trouble you? What, if anything, would be lost by such an application of technology to the assessment of students' writing?

Here is Carr's concern:

How, I wondered, would the Edexcel software discern those rare students who break from the conventions of writing not because they're incompetent but because they have a special spark of brilliance? I knew the answer: it wouldn't. Computers, as Joseph Weizenbaum pointed out, follow rules; they don't make judgments. In place of subjectivity, they give us formula. (ibid: 223–224)

The last thing we need is a formula for students' learning. Teachers can make subtle judgements and be subjective. You are not a gadget.

Students placed at the heart of their own education

We hear a lot about 'student voice' in our university. We are sure the same is true within your school. However, students do not need a voice. They already have one. What students need is much more than just the opportunity of being heard. If you have time, read Sam Levin's story in full in *The Washington Post* (Strauss 2014) for one example of how a school responded seriously to this assertion. For Sam, students need real 'agency' in their education. Here's a short quote from the end of his powerful article:

We need to give them a pen and a microphone and a hammer and a shovel and a chalkboard. We need to give them a classroom and an audience and a blank sheet that says 'curriculum' at the top. We need to give them a budget and a building. Kids are disengaged. They aren't learning, and a lot of what they *are* learning is no longer relevant to the 21st Century. Fortunately that's becoming more kosher to say. It's no longer radical; people are starting to see the problems. But unfortunately, a lot of the proposed solutions aren't radical enough. They're superficial. People talk about giving students a voice. A seat at the table. If we're going to solve these problems, we're going to need more than that. We want kids to be engaged in learning, to be excited to show up and happy about school. **Give them real agency in their own education**. (ibid; our emphasis)

When we ask to create a new unit of work for the university course that we teach, we are immediately given a template and vocabulary that describes the educational landscape and frames the possibilities for learning. The template is dominated by learning outcomes, objectives, assessment types, evaluation criteria and delivery. Within schools, the same is true. You are faced with lesson planning, units of work, and longer-term planning built around National Curriculum frameworks or examination specifications. It is very easy to imagine the kinds of conversation and debate that usher in these planning templates. They begin by asking what we want students to learn, what content we should use, and how we can best measure whether or not the learning outcomes have been met. They are exactly the same questions that frame national debates over educational policy and ideology.

They are also all the wrong questions. What would happen if, instead of:

- Focussing on outcomes and content delivery – we start by asking our students what learning experiences they want to have whilst they are in school or university?

- Shoe-horning students into curricula templates – we begin to wonder how to engage students and help them nurture their passions?

- Thinking of 'engagement' as a physical presence – we look at it as the evolving identity of a student as they practise and perform in different contexts?

- Worrying about how best to deliver content – we concentrate on working out how to use our network resources and social connections to bring people who want to learn together?

- Paying lip-service to the 'student voice' – we give them real agency in their own learning by providing the tools and the curriculum to make their institutions really student-centred?

- Being blind to the idea that school is just one node in a network of learning for you, me and our students – we opened our eyes to the idea that expertise is widely distributed in our society and that it's not only teachers who can help someone get better at something?

When Mae Holland is lucky enough to be offered a job at The Circle (Eggers 2013), she throws herself into the maelstrom that is the office of Customer Experience. A 'Zing' account is opened for her. Zinging is an amalgamation of Tweeting, texting and pinging, and is a common form of communication on the 'campus' where The Circle has built a series of connected glass-fronted buildings housing the brightest minds of its generation. Mae's performance is measured by her approval ratings on network activities: the number of zings she deals with, the 'smiles' and 'frowns' she relays across the network, and her 'participation rank' in the numerous company groups that vie for her attention. Mae is always on, always connected to the company, to the network, and always measurable. Her three and later four screens are a constant flow of network activity – feeds from her customers, her co-workers, and her social participation in the company.

She soon realises how well she could perform in this hyper-connected world. She's driven to want to know everything, to be at the centre, a super-connector, one of an elite, able to track, absorb and re-distribute those interminable flows of information that form the network. One night she tries to scale the heights of T2K (the nickname for the top 2,000 Circlers), to become one of the elite. Mae's single-minded pursuit of excellence is described as a drift into a kind of mania:

> The total number of stats she was tracking was only 41. There was her aggregate customer service score, which was at 97. There was her last score, which was 99. There was the average of her pod, which was at 96. There was the number of queries handled that day thus far, 221, and the number of queries handled by that time yesterday, 219, and the number handled by her on average, 220, and by the pod's other members: 198. (Eggers 2013: 157)

It's the score that matters. Mae begins to realise that her ability to 'multi-track' as many indexes of her own existence and self-worth could be her salvation. She turns to her second screen: it's the score that matters.

> There was the number of friends in Mae's OuterCircle, 762, and outstanding requests by those wanting to be her friend, 27. There were the number of zingers she was following, 10,343, and the number following her, 18,198. There was the number of unread zings, 887. There was the number of zingers suggested to her, 12,862. (ibid)

The quest to track all this is bordering on the absurd, but Mae remains convinced that the goal is achievable. She just has to monitor herself as her digital life streams across her various screens: 33,002 images in her digital library and 100,038 others for her to look at recommended by those in her circles; 6,877 songs in her digital collection by 921 artists. The numbers are insistent, threatening even in their precision, unerring accuracy and capacity to update constantly. Can Mae really keep up? Can we? In the world of The Circle nothing is approximate. Look now and see the exact numbers. Look in five minutes time and there are new numbers, equally precise. This is the digital world driven by 0s and 1s. If T. S. Eliot's Prufrock measured his life in coffee spoons, then Mae measures hers in bits and bytes.

The Circle is a work of fiction, a satire on our present obsessions and future dystopia. However, in its description of how the dreams of social connectivity can turn into a nightmare, it reminds us all about that technology-driven mentality which suggests that through constantly watching, monitoring and commenting we could somehow know everything. If you haven't read it, we won't spoil it for you by revealing the plot and its denouement. What we will say, though, is that the message is clear: boundary-less communication and total transparency lead to total control by the owners of information.

Summary

This chapter takes an alternative look at technology in education. It touches on a number of key sceptical messages and introduces a range of writing from various authors who are all questioning the received wisdom of technological progress being solely beneficial. It urges you to question things and not to make assumptions about your use of technology within teaching. It seeks to reassert the role of the skilful teacher as a key communicator and wise decision maker in respect of the tools that are used within the school. It reminds you that there should be clear boundaries within the school about when technology should and should not be used. These boundaries should be underpinned by a robust understanding of what technology can and cannot achieve. Finally, we have explored the importance of ensuring students are placed at the heart of our work as educators. Prioritising student voice is not what is required. We need to take students, and their aspirations for their education, seriously and place them right at the centre of our curriculum development process.

Teachers need to be wise, critical and cautious in their use of technology. To do otherwise, can spell disaster. From his teenage years, Nicholas Carr recalls watching Stanley Kubrick's classic film *2001: A Space Odyssey*. Towards the end of the film, the spaceship's computer, HAL, responds to the disassembly of its mind thus – 'I can feel it, I can feel it. I'm afraid.' This contrasts strongly with the emotionless, robotic efficiency of the human figures in the film.

Carr comments:

In the world of *2001*, people have become so machinelike that the most human character turns out to be a machine. That's the essence of Kubrick's dark prophecy: as we come to rely on computers to mediate our understanding of the world, it is our own intelligence that flattens into artificial intelligence. (Carr 2010: 224)

This is a stark picture of everything that our educational system should not become.

Notes

1   This title is 'borrowed' from Lanier (2011).
2   www.khanacademy.org
3   moodle.com
4   webct.com

References

Alexander, R. J. (2008). *Essays on Pedagogy*. London, Routledge.
Barnwell, P. (2014). 'My students don't know how to have a conversation'. *The Atlantic*, 22 April. www.theatlantic.com/education/archive/2014/04/my-students-dont-know-how-to-have-a-conversation/360993 [last accessed 1/8/14].

Bauerlein, M. (2008). *The Dumbest Generation: How the digital age stupefies young Americans and jeopardizes our future.* New York, Penguin.

Bilton, N. (2013). 'The child, the tablet and the developing mind'. *The New York Times*, 31 March. bits.blogs.nytimes.com/2013/03/31/disruptions-what-does-a-tablet-do-to-the-childs-mind [last accessed 4/8/14].

Carr, N. (2010). *The Shallows: How the internet is changing the way we think, read and remember.* London, Atlantic Books.

Eggers, D. (2013). *The Circle.* London, Penguin Books.

Eliot, T. S. (2001). *Prufrock and other observations.* London, Faber.

Garber, M. (2014). 'Saving the lost art of conversation'. *The Atlantic*, Jan/Feb. www.theatlantic.com/magazine/archive/2014/01/the-eavesdropper/355727 [last accessed 4/8/14].

Herbert, M. (2000). *Selected Poems of T. S. Eliot: York Notes Advanced.* London, Longman.

Lanier, J. (2011). *You Are Not a Gadget: A manifesto.* London, Penguin Books.

Lawler, P. (2013). 'Is This Both the Smartest and the Dumbest Generation?', *The Big Think*. bigthink.com/rightly-understood/is-this-both-the-smartest-and-dumbest-generation-3 [last accessed 1/8/14].

Morozov, E. (2013). *To Save Everything, Click Here: The folly of technological solutionism.* London, Penguin.

Ratcliffe, R. (2014). 'Eton Headmaster: England's exam system unimaginative and outdated'. *The Guardian*, 5 August. www.theguardian.com/education/2014/aug/05/eton-headmaster-exam-system-unimaginative [last accessed 5/8/14].

Strauss, V. (2014). 'Students don't need a "voice." Here's what they really need', www.washingtonpost.com/blogs/answer-sheet/wp/2014/04/16/students-dont-need-a-voice-heres-what-they-really-need [last accessed 1/8/14].

Talbert, R. (2012). 'The Trouble with Khan Academy'. chronicle.com/blognetwork/castingoutnines/2012/07/03/the-trouble-with-khan-academy/ [last accessed 4/8/4].

Turkle, S. (2011). *Alone Together: Why we expect more from technology and less from each other.* New York, Basic Books.

6 Developing a networked approach to education

KEY QUESTIONS

- What have been the key concepts that we have covered in the book to this point?
- How can you adopt a process of education evaluation within your work to help investigate a networked approach to teaching and learning within your classroom?

A quick review

Congratulations on reaching the final chapter of our book! We hope you have found it an enjoyable and productive read. We have travelled a long road together. It began with us considering the nature of creativity, and how the orthodox view of creativity being the sole remit of a creative mind tells only half the story at best. Creativity is social. It's shared. Creativity occurs when people connect to each other in various ways. As Johnson (2010: 22) says, 'chance favours the connected mind'. We also explored how creative people work with 'stuff'. They do not start with a blank piece of paper. Creative borrowing – stealing – is integral to the creative process. Do you remember the quote from Austin Kleon, sourced originally from T. S. Eliot?

> Immature poets imitate; mature poets steal; bad poets deface what they take, and good poets make it into something better, or at least something different. (Kleon 2012:4)

The processes of combining and re-mixing materials are not the preserve of artists alone. All creative people, whatever their discipline, are collaborators. Teachers are no exception. You will need to connect, borrow, combine, re-mix and collaborate in order to become the best teacher that you can be. We considered how these thoughts relate to two key educational activities: reading and writing.

In Chapter 2 we explored how networks of varying types provide the infrastructure through which this social creative process can flourish. Beginning with Harry Beck's map of the London Underground, we saw how the mapping of networks can help spark new ideas, re-imagine or re-visualise common components of a system and spark new connections. Moreno's work taught us that our relationships with others are part of a complex socio-emotional networking that can have all kinds of desirable, and not so desirable, consequences. As every teacher knows, the dynamic with every class of students is very different. Even if you break the class up into smaller groups for a particular activity, every group will be different. This is one of the reasons why teaching is such an engaging and enjoyable activity. Every class, every group, every student is different.

Caldarelli, drawing on Moreno's work, taught us a very important lesson. It is in the patterns of interaction where the richest information about an organisation lies. For us, the richest information about our students is in their interactions, their behaviour, language (spoken, written and otherwise), organisation, emotional response, off-the-cuff comments, jokes, banter, discussion, and so much more that you can observe on a daily basis within any classroom. This is where their learning is located.

But networks extend well beyond the classroom and the school into a much wider array. However, as work in the USA by Stanley Milgram, Granovetter and others has shown us, the world is actually smaller than we might think. Numerous studies have proved the concept that we are closely connected to our fellow human beings and that super-connectors play an important part within those networks. Watts and Strogatz, building on the work done by others, have shown that within our contemporary experience of the world, connection is more important than distance. We considered some famous networks and noticed how things spread through them quickly. On the positive side, being connected to happy people within a social network will result in you being more happy, and the closer the degree of connection, the greater the impact of their happiness on you. Sadly, the same is also true for more negative things, too.

Castell's work, introduced in the final part of Chapter 2, documents how networks have replaced machines as the organising principle and metaphor through which we understand how society works. An industrial revolution has been followed by a technological revolution, within which digital tools have allowed a degree of connectedness that it would have been very difficult to anticipate even twenty-five years ago. The affordances of the web have challenged many aspects of education and its organisation, not least what counts as 'knowledge' and how it might be best delivered. Drawing on Castell's work, leading educational theorists such as George Siemens and Stephen Downes have explored how learning can be refashioned for this networked society. Their theory of connectivism is a new learning theory for the digital age. It is characterised by an inherent diversity that no single person can control. Learning becomes a process of connecting dots between silos of information sets, and is best done through cooperation and collaboration. The ability to sort and curate information becomes a core skill, as does the ability to evaluate information quickly. Given our limited mental capacity, the tools we use to store information and retrieve it when needed have developed and changed rapidly in recent times. Our ability to connect to the web at will is challenging notions of what it is important for us to know and remember ourselves.

In Chapter 3 we explored the concept of sharing as a form of social exchange. We noted that we are more likely to share our knowledge, skills and experiences when we are fully integrated into a network that is rich in social capital. The secret to increasing social capital within a network is trust and norms of reciprocity: if we can't agree how to share, how to give and take, or if we don't trust the people, organisations or other elements within our network and have no mechanisms for measuring that trust, then we are all going to be much poorer.

We looked at the range of reasons why people share, as well as some of the characteristics or hallmarks of successful sharing strategies. Sharing, of course, is one way of describing what we do as teachers. We share knowledge; we share skills within our subject disciplines; we share an approach to and engagement with life itself with our students. Sharing, within education, is the way we share values that are important to us all within our local communities and broader society.

One of the most positive ways we can respond as teachers is through the construction of a personal learning network. We looked at what this might entail. We defined what we mean by this term and related it to a set of core web competencies that will help you develop your own personal learning network effectively. We discussed a range of behaviours that a personal learning network will facilitate (including how you explore the web, search for information, follow sources that are of interest, monitor and tune your network; and most importantly, how you engage with others, enquiring and responding in a positive manner). We also looked at a number of personal learning networks and identified their core elements and the tools around which they are built. We emphasised the key point that these networks extend beyond the web and embrace a range of other people and organisations in our everyday lives.

Within a sharing network, the act of curation is central to engagement. In the final part of Chapter 3, we saw how the term curation has developed over the years and how its practice, and the values that underpin it, relate to our work as educators. In the digital age, the sheer amount of information that heads your way can be overwhelming. You will need clear strategies to organise and curate it. Similarly, your role as teacher will be to help educate your students in the art of digital curation, of being able to collect content quickly, search through and personalise that content for a specific purpose (such as a particular lesson or curriculum topic), share it in a format suitable for your students, and facilitate a discussion around it (both within and outside formal lessons).

In Chapter 4, we turned our attention more explicitly to pedagogical aspects. As teachers, how should we be responding to this digital revolution? We considered the teaching and learning approaches that you might adopt within the networked classroom. We looked at how approaches to building knowledge can be transformed through a personal learning network. We also considered how elements of your teaching style and role might be developed as you begin to embrace these new approaches.

The final part of Chapter 4 explored partnership approaches to education within your classroom. We made the obvious point that all teaching is about partnership in a general sense, before looking briefly at alternative approaches to partnership working and curriculum development using your local area as a resource. We moved on to look at how partnership approaches can be developed both within and across subjects in interesting ways, noting the prevalence of digital tools (of various types depending on their historical context), and drew on the work of other artists (the electro-acoustic composer) to explore further how education with technology truly is underpinned by collaborative or networked partnership working.

Chapter 5 provided a different, more sceptical perspective on digital technology and our networked culture. It explored the consequences of the rapid adoption of these tools and identified a number of key things we might be losing as a result. Central to these concerns was Morozov's notion of 'technological solutionism', the strategy of jumping onto simple technological solutions to problems before knowing exactly what those problems are and how they might be framed and understood (Morozov 2013). Sadly, this concept is only too evident in the schools and universities that we visit and work within. We looked at a number of common tools that are in use within education today, and gave a contrary viewpoint to that often espoused by manufacturers and others wanting to make a quick buck. We asked some fundamental questions about what students really need (rather than what they want), and reinforced the view that skilful teachers make skilful decisions about the tools they use, which they can justify on pedagogical grounds when required. The chapter closed with a call to take 'student voice' seriously and at face value, rather than merely seeking to superimpose what we, as teachers, consider to be the voice that we presume students need.

Having got this far into our book, perhaps the time is right to begin to make a more explicit link back to the main context of your work – the classroom. The concept of a reflective practitioner is a common one in courses of initial teacher education. Having a reflective or an evaluative 'eye' is vital in making improvements to your teaching, lesson-by-lesson and term-by-term. In the final part of this book, we will guide you through a simple process by which you can take some of the ideas of this book and apply them to your work as a teacher through a structured piece of evaluation.

Exploring your pedagogy through a structured piece of evaluation

It is not enough that teachers' work should be studied; they need to study it themselves. (Stenhouse 1975: 143)

Enquiry counts as research to the extent that it is systematic, but even more to the extent that it can claim to be conscientiously self-critical. (Stenhouse 1985: 15)

Evaluation is integral to the process of learning to become a teacher. For us, like Stenhouse, the process of evaluating the curriculum that we are offering to our students is embedded within the day-to-day work of a skilful teacher. In what follows, we are principally going to talk about a one-off evaluation designed for the purposes of evaluating any changes that you would like to make to your teaching in light of the issues explored throughout this book. But the skills that educational evaluation entails are intricately linked to the general skills required to be an effective teacher. For that reason, evaluation (in either a general or a specific sense) is something that you will quickly become good at if you practise it regularly.

Education is complicated. You know this better than anyone else. Watching education in action within a classroom or other learning environment is fascinating.

REFLECTIVE TASK

Before reading ahead any further, take a moment to pause. What are the first few things that come into your head when you hear the word 'evaluation'?

What do you consider to be the differences between evaluation, assessment and reflection?

Educational evaluation can help you understand more fully the activities that go on within your classroom. Like Stenhouse's view of educational research, evaluation is a tool that you can use to investigate your own practice in a systematic and self-critical way. It can also be an approach that teams of educators could employ to investigate specific pieces of curriculum development. One of the key benefits of adopting a process of educational evaluation within your work will be to allow you to ascertain the value of adopting some of the concepts, tools and techniques related to a networked approach to teaching and learning within your classroom.

Evaluation has many aspects. As we have mentioned, it is a very practical activity that sits well within your portfolio of work as a teacher. It includes looking at things, asking questions, listening to others, describing events and making interpretations. It is a skilful activity. Some people talk about it as an art form.

Designing an evaluation

Although this curriculum development project might be a fictitious entity in your mind at the moment, the issues outlined below will be equally applicable whether the work is centred within your own teaching practice or is situated as part of a wider, collaborative project with other members of staff in your department or school.

Choose a unit of work that you are going to be teaching in the following few months. As a one-off activity, use the advice below about educational evaluation to conduct a study of your teaching of this unit. Working collaboratively with another colleague in your school would make this a more meaningful activity. You would not necessarily need to agree on all the fine detail of the planned curriculum, but you could use your colleague as another source of inspiration and ideas, eyes and ears and, where possible, ask them to visit your classroom to assist in providing feedback to you about teaching during this unit of work. Perhaps you could return the favour if they were to do a similar study of their own? See if you can forge such a relationship with a colleague.

Here are some key principles at this planning stage that should underpin your work.

Right at the outset, commit to being a creative and reflective teacher

As with all aspects of teaching and learning, creativity and an ability to be reflective are key hallmarks of effective curriculum development of this sort and any accompanying evaluation. Planning can sometimes feel like a rather dry exercise. It shouldn't be! In both, you will want to build in opportunities for creativity (on your part as the teacher and for your students) and reflective practice (again, for both you and the students) in order to understand more deeply the impact the curriculum is having on your teaching and their learning.

Establish the wider context of your evaluation and share your evaluation's design

Start any evaluation by trying to define the wider context of your proposed curriculum development. This could involve a number of different activities. First of all, have similar pieces of curriculum development been undertaken elsewhere? If you don't have the time to do significant searching of written or electronic sources, posting a short question on a teachers' website/forum (such as the *Times Educational Supplement*) may be worthwhile. Local authority advisers can often have a helpful overview of work that is going on in different schools. Universities with education departments may also be a useful point of contact. Having read this book is a great start to this process. You can draw on your personal learning network for ideas and inspiration, get feedback from other people or organisations that you are connected to, and share your thinking at all stages.

This leads on to the second key point. Sharing your curriculum unit and the accompanying evaluation framework at an early stage is important. Who might you share this with? In the context of a piece of school-based curriculum development, we would urge you to share your ideas with the senior manager within your school who has a responsibility for the curriculum at the appropriate Key Stage. Whilst this might have an effect on the political dimension of your work (you probably don't want to upset your senior managers), as you are working within a management system where accountability is important, they probably have a right to know what is going on. But, more importantly than that, by sharing your ideas and design at this early stage you are showing yourself to be a reflective teacher, someone who is serious about wanting to initiate change in their teaching in a systematic and responsible way.

More informally, of course, there will be many other folk to whom you are connected through your personal learning network who will be interested in what you are doing. They will provide you with ideas and support that you will find hard to imagine. You've constructed your network – now use it!

Set out the aims, outcomes and activities of the evaluation

You will be used to setting aims and objectives for units of work and lesson plans. All teaching involves the design of creative and engaging teaching activities through which students can learn the key objectives you have set. Skilful teachers are able to predict what some of these are through their planning, but also to be responsive and alert during their lessons and to develop these in light of how students are responding. As any teacher will tell you, students often learn things along the way that you haven't anticipated.

The skills you have developed in all these contexts can be applied to the design of a piece of educational evaluation. You will need to ask yourself general and specific questions about the purpose of the evaluation and what you hope it will achieve. We would strongly recommend that these relate in some way to the broader teaching and learning objectives that you have set.

Building links between the activities of the curriculum unit and the accompanying evaluation is also a good idea. Typical activities within the unit itself will include various pedagogical elements that you have bought together to promote the learning you want students to engage with. Use these activities to assist in the process of the educational evaluation; in other words, position the activities of the evaluation, whatever they might be (and we give you three options to consider below), within the teaching activities in an integrated way. Ensuring the evaluation is embedded within the curriculum unit, rather than being bolted onto the end of it, is the best way.

Think about this in relation to how you assess your students' work. Assessment is always better when it is an integral part of the teaching and learning process rather than being conceptualised and delivered as a separate activity within the classroom.

Manage the resources within your evaluation

Thinking about the resources of your evaluation will require you to consider a range of issues. Firstly, and perhaps most importantly, decide on the amount of time you have to devote to the evaluation of the unit. Doubtless there will be a whole range of other things that you have to do during the course of an average teaching day. Things need to be manageable. Even if you have limited time, try to allow for a regular period of time during the evaluation for reflection. This is better than spending a lot of time at the beginning and end of the project, with nothing or very little in between.

Although an evaluation of a curriculum unit of this type could be done as an individual venture, perhaps the benefit of collaboration is most keenly felt here. Working with a colleague on a piece of curriculum development has many advantages, not least in sharing the workload, and having that sense of a shared journey through a new educational landscape.

In addition to time, there will be other resources that you can use to assist your evaluation. We would strongly recommend the use of portable audio and video technologies to help you capture key moments within the unit. Much of this could be facilitated with simple software on a computer, tablet or mobile device. Again, involve your students in this. Asking them to reflect on their work in progress via reviewing a video of themselves working can be a fascinating experience for student and teacher alike. We will return to this in greater detail below.

Similarly, build in key questions that relate to your evaluation in written feedback that your students could provide through their exercise books or folders. Anything that helps you capture an essence or flavour of their work in the unit will help you form a more detailed understanding at a later date. This moves us directly onto our next point, data collection.

Collect a range of data about your curriculum unit

Collecting data sounds very grand. In practice, it can be quite simple. Aim to collect data related to the evaluation of your curriculum unit on a regular basis. Remember that evaluative data, like assessment data, can take many shapes and forms. You may have chosen a particular class, or group of pupils within a class, to be the specific focus for evaluation of the unit. Whatever you do, keep it manageable and within the allocation of time that you have decided to devote to the evaluation. You might consider keeping a teaching journal for the duration of the evaluation. This could contain short comments about teaching sessions, notes about your thoughts or feelings during the evaluation process, snapshots of conversations with students, or other things that come to your mind and might be useful later on. This kind of reflective writing can be an invaluable aspect of your evaluation. You will find many other published resources to assist with this aspect of evaluation or more structured pieces of educational research (e.g. McNiff 2005; McIntosh 2010; Phillips and Carr 2010).

Three key activities within your evaluation

Your unit of work has been written. You have identified your aims and objectives, chosen your curriculum activities, selected the classes you are going to work with, set a time-scale to work within and established your available resources. You have shared your ideas with your senior manager and other selected colleagues, and reflected on their advice. You're ready to go. So, what are you actually going to do during the evaluation itself? What are the activities that you can undertake, alongside your teaching, to help collect the data you need to understand more fully the impact of a networked approach to teaching and learning in your classroom?

In this part of the chapter we explore three key activities that you can undertake, which are complementary to your teaching role. This complementarity is crucial. Finding the links between teaching and evaluation will help you manage your time effectively and avoid you being distracted from your key role as a teacher in your classroom. It will also make for a better evaluation and assist you in your own development as a teacher. The three activities are:

- Observation;

- Communication;

- Interviewing.

Observing your classroom

As teachers, we are used to observing classrooms. It is a key aspect of our work. Effective teachers make time during their lessons to take that step backwards from their teaching role, and the complexity of the classroom interactions that are occurring between themselves and their students, to observe what is going on. Using observation as a key component of your evaluation will greatly enhance your generic teaching abilities.

There is a flip side to this. Familiarity with the classroom can be a barrier to effective observation. Therefore it will be important to find ways to challenge your own observations, particularly if you are conducting this evaluative work within your own teaching. To this end, we briefly consider a range of issues associated with observation that will help you to do this.

Firstly, learn to live with uncertainty in your observations. It is quite right and understandable that, on occasions, you will not be able to make immediate sense of what is going on. As we explored above, the notion of 'truth' within an evaluation is highly contestable. What you are watching is framed by notions of objectivity and subjectivity which you could spend a lifetime exploring. You don't have time to do that now. Rather, look for examples of activities that are 'credible and defensible rather that true' (Kushner 1992a: 1). Subtleties in your observations can be explored at a later date through the second and third activities discussed below. Whilst you are observing, use your instincts as a teacher to look out for interesting responses that your students make within the lesson, unusual responses within particular activities, or that spark of creativity that a student may show at a given moment. Accounting for these in a simple way through your observation notes will be important, even if it's just a brief comment in your teaching journal that can be returned to at a later date.

Secondly, use a range of technologies to help you with your observations. As we mentioned above, this could include audio or video recording. The review and analysis of these materials can also reveal interesting material that you may miss in the hurly-burly of a lesson. Whilst this can be a timesaver and assist you in conducting the dual roles of teacher and evaluator, beware of relying too much on recording. It takes a long time to review recorded materials, and you may not have much time available, given your other commitments. But the benefits can be significant if you have the time. In acting, dancing and athletics, video analysis is central to improving performance. Why should it be any different for teachers?

Finally, be focussed in your observations. Your unit has specific aims and objectives. Try and focus on these in the early stages of your observation. But, as we discussed above, remember that these aims and objectives should not be thought of as being set in stone. They will develop as the piece of curriculum development unfolds, and you will need to be responsive to the outworking of these throughout the curriculum activities that you have designed.

Communicating effectively

Like observation, communication is a vital component of effective teaching and learning. Communication can take many forms, and you will need to be alert for these throughout your evaluation. Non-verbal forms of communication, such as gesture, body language or facial expression, will all be evident within your classroom. But verbal communication will probably be a major focus in all evaluations. In particular, conversations between teachers and students are an essential part of every classroom context, and present a vital opportunity for the evaluation. How can we use the opportunities to converse with students to help the process of your evaluation?

Firstly, be as natural as you can be in your conversations with students. Clearly, you are still their teacher and this will frame your conversations at a certain level. But build on your existing relationship with the class, or the individual student, and seek to nurture conversations around your key evaluation aims and objectives. Try to do this in a natural, not a forced, way. Do your students need to know that you are evaluating a particular approach to curriculum design within these lessons? There will be differences of opinion on this point, but if you feel this is going to close down their responses (you think they're going to say what they think you want to hear), then we would suggest not.

Secondly, take nothing for granted. Listen to the conversations that students are having between themselves during the various activities that you have designed within the curriculum unit. Make it your practice not to interrupt them too soon. These conversations often contain really important evidence that can usefully inform your evaluation. When you do intervene, maintain a critical stance and don't close down the possibilities for them to express alternative viewpoints.

Thirdly, don't over-depend on the students' voices and forget your own. As we saw in the previous chapter, 'student voice' is a problematic term that many educationalists are now finding unhelpful. For some, the emphasis on student voice is nothing more than adult's 'copping out' and an 'abdication of their responsibilities' (Paton 2009). Whilst we cannot completely agree with this perspective, it is important to remember that your viewpoint and opinion does matter. So, don't underplay what *you* think about your own and your students' work in your evaluation.

Interviewing students

The final key activity for your evaluation ought to be interviewing. Interviewing has a long history in educational research and it can prove to be a very beneficial approach within evaluations too. There are many guides on how to conduct interviews with young people, either within educational research (Kvale 2007) or as part of a clinical setting (Ginsburg 1997). There are a number of important points to consider here.

Firstly, interviews that are mainly about information-retrieval make a number of assumptions. They assume that the interviewee (in our case, the student) knows something that the interviewer (that's you) doesn't know. The task of the interview is to extract that information. Your role might be to put that particular student or students at ease, asking them appropriate questions and facilitating the resulting conversation in a way that exposes the information that is deemed important. This is a perfectly legitimate approach to interviewing and one that, given the potential resource constraints that you may find yourself facing, may be the best use of your time.

However, there is a second way in which interviews can be conducted that may be even more beneficial. The 'developmental interview' is underpinned by a range of different assumptions. As Kushner explains:

> This approach assumes that interviewee probably does not know either and the task of the interviewer is to set up a learning situation. The interviewee is seen as someone locked up in a role and unable to take an objective role of what he or she knows, so the task of the interview is to prise the person out of the role and to ask them to look back at it and evaluate it. The interview is typified by exploration, by asking many supplementary questions to clarify and extend an idea. [...] The focus is on the individual rather than the project – their life and values. The idea is to see the project in the context of the person's life. (Kushner 1992b: 1)

This approach to interviewing is more time-consuming. But, as Kushner points out in a later point in his exposition, it can be conducted over a longer period, perhaps as an interview that takes place on a number of separate occasions or stages. For teachers, this type of dialogue with a student could become part of the design of a one-off evaluation of the type we have discussed throughout this chapter. By asking the right sorts of questions, students could engage with this type of focus through written responses as well as in a face-to-face interview. This may also be less threatening from their perspective, and certainly less time-consuming from your point of view. We really like the dual emphasis of using the interview for some kind of joint exploration with the student, or students, as well as being an educational experience for all involved.

This moves us on to a final point about interviewing. If you are going to include interviewing in your evaluation (and we would encourage you to), try and give it a sense of occasion from the students' perspective. In our own evaluation work as teachers, we would often try and find opportunities outside the formal time of a lesson to talk to students about their work. This might include changing a formal interview into more of a lunchtime 'focus group', where students can relax and eat their lunch, and you can talk about their work on a particular project. We found that this was more relaxing for us, too. Group interviews or focus groups of this sort are often better and result in a better quality of information for you to consider. Students can bounce their ideas off each other and, when this is going well, you can often find yourself taking a back seat in the interview process. This is a good sign that the interview is moving beyond the 'information-retrieval' approach and really entering a developmental, formative educational phase.

Drawing conclusions

You have reached the end of the evaluation period. You have observed students working through what you have planned and delivered, you have talked to them about their work, conducted group interviews with a selected number of students, and completed a teaching journal throughout the evaluation. In a parallel stream of activity, perhaps, you have being assessing your students' work in formative and summative ways. Your assessment data are collated and organised, and you have been able to provide the appropriate top-level assessment data to your senior manager. You are faced with a collection of data drawn from your assessment and evaluative processes. It is time to make some judgments about how this new unit of work has helped you adopt a networked approach to teaching and learning in your classroom.

One of the key ways of making judgements in this situation is to ask yourself questions about the data you have collected. Perhaps this is easier when you are working collaboratively, but it is certainly possible to do this individually. The following types of question may be useful to consider at this moment.

■ Was this the appropriate time for a piece of curriculum development for me (as a teacher), for my students, my department and my school? How can I be sure?

■ What are the consequences of the changes I have made for myself, my students and my colleagues?

- How do the changes I have advocated relate to other changes that we are being asked to make?

- Where do the values come from that underpin this piece of curriculum development? Are they from my experiences or beliefs, or are they from somewhere else? If so, can I pinpoint precisely where they originated?

- Who have been the winners and losers in this piece of curriculum development?

- How has the teaching and learning been connected in this piece of curriculum development? How do I know?

- How would I describe the teaching approach I have adopted throughout this curriculum unit? Has it been authoritarian or democratic, formal or informal? What aspects of my pedagogy have changed or developed from my traditional, subject-based pedagogy?

- How have my students learnt in this project? How is this different from ways of learning that might have been in evidence in a more traditional approach to the same topic? What have I learnt from the whole experience?

- Were my original aims, objectives and activities for the curriculum unit appropriate? Did they change or develop over the duration of the unit?

- Whose knowledge really counts within a piece of curriculum development like this? How did the knowledge base of my own subject(s) or phase relate to the unit I had planned?

- If this was a piece of curriculum development that I did on my own, would it have worked better as a piece of collaborative curriculum development? If it was collaborative in its structure, can I conceive of it working more effectively as an independent activity? Could the collaborative dimensions of the project be translated into an individual teacher's pedagogical approach?

These questions may or may not be appropriate for the piece of curriculum development you have undertaken. Learning to ask the right questions about your work is part of the process of reaching a judgment about the project. It may be that you could adapt some of the above questions for your own work. You may need to invent your own.

This questioning process may continue for some time. Pragmatically, you are going to have to draw a line under this at some point and move forward. But reaching a conclusion, in your mind or as a written report of the evaluation, is an important final step. We would encourage you to write up the evaluation, however briefly, as an integral part of this process. For Stenhouse (1983), educational research was 'systematic enquiry made public'. The making public part of this definition is crucial, partly because it provides a system of accountability but, more importantly, because making your findings public will help create a dialogue of ideas about teaching and learning that will benefit yourself and others.

So, as a final part of this evaluative process, submit a short report to your senior managers, but also look out for opportunities to share your work with other teachers. The findings from your study could be shared through your personal learning network. You could also prepare a short piece of writing that extrapolates some implications for the work of other teachers. Again, share this through your personal learning network. Blog about it. Tweet about it. Find similar studies from other teachers, and comment on their work in light of what you have found out for yourself. Engage in a dialogue and conversation with others about your project. It will make it all seem worthwhile – and you will almost certainly gain more out of this than you have to give.

This type of approach empowers the individual teacher. In a political era of top-down educational initiatives, it reasserts the authority of the teacher and places them at the centre of the process of curriculum development. It does take time, but it is time richly rewarded for you and your students.

Some final words

Clearly, a printed book of this type is very much an old technology. Whilst some of you will have read this as an ebook, the flow of information is pretty one-sided – from us to you. However, we are both genuinely interested in finding out more about your work in this area and how it is developing. We are easily contactable through Manchester Metropolitan University, where we work. We are also both available on Twitter (which, for us, is an integral part of our own personal learning networks at the current time). Jonathan is @jpjsavage and Clive is @waldenpond. Please get in touch with your comments, thoughts and ideas. We will look forward to hearing from you.

For now, why don't you spend a few moments completing the following short Practical Task and sharing the results through your own personal learning network? Good luck with all your teaching as part of a vibrant networked society.

PRACTICAL TASK

In 140 characters or less, summarise the key learning that this book has helped you develop. Tweet your thoughts to the world, and make sure you copy us in so we can respond enthusiastically!

References

Ginsburg, H. P. (1997). *Entering the Child's Mind: The clinical interview in psychological research and practice.* Cambridge, Cambridge University Press.

Johnson, S. (2010). *Where Good Ideas Come From: The natural history of innovation.* New York, Riverhead Books.

Kleon, A. (2010). *Newspaper Blackout.* New York, Harper Perennial.

Kleon, A. (2012). *Steal Like an Artist: 10 things nobody told you about being creative.* New York, Workman.

Kushner, S. (1992a). 'Section 5: Making observations', in *The Arts, Education and Evaluation: An introductory pack with practical exercises.* Norwich, Centre for Applied Research in Education, University of East Anglia.

Kushner, S. (1992b). 'Section 6: Interviewing', in *The Arts, Education and Evaluation: An introductory pack with practical exercises.* Norwich, Centre for Applied Research in Education, University of East Anglia.

Kvale, S. (2007). *Doing Interviews.* London, Sage.

McIntosh, P. (2010). *Action Research and Reflective Practice.* London, Routledge.

McNiff, J. (2005). *Action Research for Teachers.* London, Routledge.

Morozov, E. (2013). *To Save Everything, Click Here: The folly of technological solutionism.* London, Penguin.

Paton, G. (2009). 'Adults "Abdicating Responsibility" for Children'. www.telegraph.co.uk/education/6598138/Adults-abdicating-responsibility-for-children.html [last accessed 10/12/09].

Phillips, D. K. and Carr, K. (2010). *Becoming a Teacher through Action Research.* London, Routledge.

Stenhouse, L. (1975). *An Introduction to Curriculum Research and Development.* London, Heinemann Educational.

Stenhouse, L. (1983). 'Research is systematic enquiry made public'. *British Educational Research Journal* 9 (1): 11–20.

Stenhouse, L. (1985). *Research as a Basis for Teaching.* London, Heinemann Educational.

Appendix 1: Mozilla's web competencies

Exploring

Navigation: Using software tools to browse the web.

- Accessing the web using the common features of web browsers;
- Using hyperlinks to access a range of resources on the web;
- Reading, evaluating, and manipulating URLs;
- Recognizing the visual cues in everyday web services;
- Using browser add-ons and extensions to provide additional functionality.

Web Mechanics: Understanding the web ecosystem.

- Using and understanding the differences between URLs, IP addresses and search terms;
- Managing information from various sources on the web;
- Demonstrating the difference between the results of varying search strategies.

Search: Locating information, people and resources via the web.

- Using keywords, search operators, and keyboard shortcuts to make web searches more efficient;
- Finding real-time or time-sensitive information using a range of search techniques;
- Locating or finding desired information within search results;
- Synthesizing information found from online resources through multiple searches.

Credibility: Critically evaluating information found on the web.

- Making judgments based on technical and design characteristics to assess the credibility of information;
- Researching authorship and ownership of websites and their content;
- Comparing information from a number of sources to judge the trustworthiness of content;
- Discriminating between 'original' and derivative web content.

Security: Keeping systems, identities, and content safe.

- Detecting online scams and 'phishing' by employing recognized tools and techniques;
- Encrypting data and communications using software and add-ons;
- Changing the default behavior of websites, add-ons and extensions to make web browsing more secure.

Building

Composing for the Web: Creating and curating content for the web.

- Inserting hyperlinks into a web page;
- Embedding multimedia content into a web page;
- Creating web resources in ways appropriate to the medium/genre;
- Identifying and using HTML tags;
- Structuring a web page.

Remixing: Modifying existing web resources to create something new.

- Identifying and using openly-licensed work;
- Combining multimedia resources;
- Creating something new on the web using existing resources.

Design and Accessibility: Creating universally effective communications through web resources.

- Identifying the different parts of a web page using industry-recognized terms;
- Improving the accessibility of a web page by modifying its color scheme and markup;
- Iterating on a design after feedback from a target audience;
- Reorganizing the structure of a web page to improve its hierarchy/conceptual flow;
- Demonstrating the difference between inline, embedded and external CSS;
- Using CSS tags to change the style and layout of a web page.

Coding/scripting: Creating interactive experiences on the web.

- Explaining the differences between client-side and server-side scripting;
- Composing working loops and arrays;
- Reading and explaining the structure of code;
- Using a script framework;
- Adding code comments for clarification and attribution.

Infrastructure: Understanding the internet stack.

- Understanding and labeling the web stack;
- Explaining the differences between the web and the internet;
- Exporting and backing up your data from web services;

- Moving the place(s) where your data is hosted on the web;
- Securing your data against malware and computer criminals.

Connecting

Sharing: Creating web resources with others.

- Sharing a resource using an appropriate tool and format for the audience;
- Tracking changes made to co-created web resources;
- Using synchronous and asynchronous tools to communicate with web communities, networks and groups.

Collaborating: Providing access to web resources.

- Choosing a web tool to use for a particular contribution/collaboration;
- Co-creating web resources;
- Configuring notifications to keep up-to-date with community spaces and interactions.

Community Participation: Getting involved in web communities and understanding their practices.

- Encouraging participation in web communities;
- Using constructive criticism in a group or community setting;
- Configuring settings within tools used by online communities;
- Participating in both synchronous and asynchronous discussions;
- Expressing opinions appropriately in web discussions;
- Defining different terminology used within online communities.

Privacy: Examining the consequences of sharing data online.

- Identifying rights retained and removed through user agreements;
- Taking steps to secure non-encrypted connections;
- Explaining ways in which computer criminals are able to gain access to user information;
- Managing the digital footprint of an online persona;
- Identifying and taking steps to keep important elements of identity private.

Open Practices: Helping to keep the web democratic and universally accessible.

- Distinguishing between open and closed licensing;
- Making web resources available under an open license;
- Using and sharing files in open, web-friendly formats when appropriate;
- Contributing to an Open Source project.

Mozilla (2014). 'Web Literacy Map (1.1.0)'.
webmaker.org/en-US/literacy [last accessed 21/7/14].

Appendix 2: Tools for creating a personal learning network

In this appendix we consider some of the most common tools that you could use to help build a personal learning network of your own. We have tried and tested all the following tools and found them to be useful core components of our work as educators. Clearly, you will make your own choices, but we highly recommend the following tools, which are all accessible and usable from desktop and mobile technologies. For each tool, we have listed some of the key behaviours that the tool will help you develop within your personal learning network.

Your web browser: the most important choice for exploring, searching and connecting

Your web browser is probably the most important tool in your personal learning network. It is your interface with the web, and probably the one piece of software that you will spend more time looking at than anything else. Each web browser has its own strengths and weaknesses. There are numerous sites online that will help you make an informed choice here, and it is not our place to recommend one browser above another (although, for the record and since you are asking, Clive uses Firefox and Jonathan uses Safari).

When choosing a browser, there are a number of key questions and options that you will want to consider:

- What is the best browser for speed?
- What is the best browser for add-ons and functionality?
- What is the best browser in terms of the other software that I have on my computer or mobile device (e.g. Windows, Mac OS, etc.)?
- What is the best browser in terms of the hardware that I am using?
- What is the best browser in terms of the privacy that it affords?
- Increasingly, for the immediate future, what is the best browser in terms of its compliance with HTML5 and the affordances this will offer for future online applications?

Whatever browser you choose, there will be opportunities for you to personalise it to your own specific requirements. You can do this through the incorporation of add-ons and bookmarklets. These might include applications from other tools within the personal learning network (e.g. an Evernote web clipper) or bespoke applications in their own right (e.g. Zotero, a research tool that allows you to collect, organise and share online content simply).

Twitter (www.twitter.com): exploring, following and engaging

Twitter has become one of the most powerful online tools. Its applications are far too numerous for us to explore here, but its core strength is its ability to easily connect people and their ideas together in short fragments of text, image or video. Twitter is, perhaps, a personal learning network all on its own, and all of the behaviour traits that we have explored above are relevant to its use. However, for us it's just one part of a wider selection of tools that you will need to adopt.

WordPress (www.wordpress.com): feeding, sharing and responding

WordPress is a content management system that has, in recent years, become a world-leading platform for bloggers. There are managed WordPress installations at sites such as www.wordpress.com, or you can host your own domain on your own server. Blogging provides you with that time and space to explore ideas and share resources without the 140 word limit imposed by Twitter. Whether through a self-hosted or managed account, the functionality offered by WordPress (and the various ways in which you can extend this through plugins) make it an essential and core part of a personal learning network.

Evernote (www.evernote.com): collecting, curating and sharing

Evernote is the ultimate digital scrapbook. It allows you to write notes, collect things like clippings from web pages, images or video, tag everything and then share it with others. It is a brilliant way to keep track of everything you need in terms of teaching resources, new ideas for curriculum development, pieces of classroom research or evaluation that you are undertaking, or materials for students to access outside your formal lessons. Evernote produces another tool, called Skitch (www.evernote.com/skitch), which allows you to annotate anything you have collected simply and easily. It has wonderful applications as a teaching tool.

Scrivener (www.literatureandlatte.com/scrivener.php): writing, curating and preparing

This book has been written using Scrivener. Many of the world's leading novelists and playwrights, journalists, lawyers and academics use Scrivener. But why is it included here as a core tool for a personal learning network?

Here's a comment from Neil Cross, the creator and writer of the BBC detective series *Luther*:

> Creating a television show is all about chaos. It doesn't matter how diligent your planning might be, things change in the writing – new connections wait to be discovered and assimilated, accelerating stories in new, more exciting directions. There are outlines, step-outlines and treatments to be written and re-written. There are producer's notes, director's notes, production notes. A million and one things can change; two million and five things actually do. A television show is alive, and it's hungry. I continue to submit my scripts in Final Draft. But all the work that gets done leading up to that submission – all the outlining, the brainstorming, the researching, the writing, the revising, the creation of structure from chaos – that gets done in Scrivener, the best writer's application in the world. (Literature & Latte 2014)

Whilst reading this, we were reminded of the cognitive processes that underpin lesson planning (Savage 2014). In a similar way to how a screen writer would want to keep track of characters, plots, sub-plots, locations and themes, the learning objectives and aims that are included within a lesson plan, and that span across our units of work and curriculum maps, can all be tagged and traced within the Scrivener environment.

As a teacher, you need to undertake a lot of writing. Although you will not be writing manuscripts of 80,000 words, you will be researching and writing significant pieces of text for the purposes of lesson planning. Scrivener provides an environment where your digital collections of materials from Evernote can be presented alongside a writing environment that allows you to connect and trace ideas through its innovative tagging mechanisms. Whilst Scrivener is not free, is it definitely worth the small cost and we highly recommend it.

References

Literature & Latte (2014). 'Who Uses Scrivener?' www.literatureandlatte.com/whouses scrivener.php [last accessed 4/8/14].
Savage, J. (2014). *Lesson Planning: Key concepts and skills for teachers*. London, Routledge.

Index

Entries in italics refer to titles of documents.
Page numbers in italics refer to figures.